Cruz Novillo Logos

Published by Counter-Print

Contents

First published in 2017. Reprinted in 2021. © Counter-Print.
ISBN 978-0-9935812-3-6. Designed by Céline Leterme and Jon Dowling.
www.counter-print.co.uk

Foreword

Jon Dowling. Counter-Print.

Pepe Cruz Novillo.

Over the past few years we have published ten books on corporate identity and logo design from around the world. This has involved a huge amount of research into the subject matter, which has, in turn, uncovered many interesting studios, collectives and individuals who practice in this field. We have come across hundreds, if not thousands of designers, all of which have been included because of their talent in the field of design. Occasionally, however, we have come across a specific designer who has opened our eyes, taken our breath away or changed our perceptions of what design can be. Pepe Cruz Novillo falls into this category.

What first drew me to the work of Cruz Novillo is both the depth and breadth of his output, which spans a career of over 50 years, but also the freshness with which we see it through today's eyes. When we first started compiling our books on logo design, I liked to contrast the old and the new, hopefully turning young designers on to the work of an older generation and forcing the reader to question the background of the work they were viewing. Captioning was kept to separate pages, which aided this discovery even more. Cruz Novillo's work was the most fun to play with, as it could sit alongside great work created in any era, including today's, with modernity second to none.

This is both due to a timeless aesthetic and the fact that he has had a huge influence on contemporary designers from his native Spain, the rest of Europe and beyond. The influence of his use of geometric shapes, simple, strong line-work and a playful, illustrative aesthetic can be seen in the work of many contemporary designers and has helped in keeping his legacy alive. Pablo Martin, founding partner and Creative Director of Spanish agency, Atlas, describes Cruz Novillo as, 'a key figure in Spanish graphic design, who helped change the Spanish landscape'.

Although we shall concentrate in this book on his design of logos, he has found recognition, in a varied career, as an artist, sculptor, designer, publisher and illustrator.

4.

> "He belongs, together with Juan Gatti, to the generation of designers who have shaped Spanish design. His work is iconic, recognisable and it's everywhere."

Born José María Cruz Novillo in Cuenca in 1936, Cruz Novillo first studied law before, in 1957, beginning a career as a cartoonist at Clarín Advertising in Madrid. Shortly after he would begin to work in the field of industrial design at SEDI, promoting years later one of the first Spanish magazines specialising in design, 'Temas de Diseño', whose editor was the architect Miguel Durán Lóriga. In 1963 he was selected to form part of the team of artists for the Pavilion of Spain at the world fair in New York. By 1965 he had reached the level of Creative Director and abandoned Clarín, opening his own design studio, where he created the corporate identities of many of Spain's national institutions and companies. His work is now so ubiquitous, it has become part of the fabric of visual culture in his native Spain. He was responsible for the identity of most of the public services like the post office (Correos)[1], national police (Cuerpo Nacional de Policia)[2], railway system (Renfe)[3], and even the Peseta notes[4]. Spanish design historian, Raquel Pelta, describes Cruz Novillo as, 'an essential figure in the history of Spanish graphic design', among other reasons because, 'since the 1970s, he has created many of the country's institutional identities. He founded, together with other designers, 'Group 13', whose purpose was to dignify and promote graphic design and he was also President of the Spanish Association of Design Professionals (AEPD)'.

His studio Cruz más Cruz, that he now co-directs with his son Pepe Cruz Jnr, himself an architect, still garners praise and recognition globally, as they continue to work on high profile corporate programs for some of Spain's largest organisations. Simultaneously, a new generation of designers are falling in love with the historical output of Cruz Novillo's work and are beginning to appreciate its significance and importance to the visual landscape of Spain. Spanish designer Astrid Stavro describes Cruz Novillo as 'vaca sagrada', which translates into sacred cow. Figuratively, it means 'créme de la créme' or 'best of the best'. She continues, 'he belongs, together with Juan Gatti, to the generation of designers who have shaped Spanish design. His work is iconic, recognisable and it's everywhere'.

1.

2.

1.
Logo for Correos, the Spanish Postal Office.
—
2.
Logo for Cuerpo Nacional de Policia, the Spanish police.

3.

4.

We hope this book will offer a comprehensive guide to one facet of Cruz Novillo's output, his logo design; and in doing so prove the importance of this body of work, both to Spain and the global design community. We believe this book will provide inspiring content for any young designers entering a career in this field and those looking to explore the subject matter of Spanish corporate design.

I'll leave the last word to his son who, when speaking about why he thought his father's work was successful, stated simply that it was because, 'he is a genius. I think that many of his works are simply unbeatable. That's the reason why they endure so many decades with full force, because they are the result of bright concepts, masterfully drawn'.

Jon Dowling
Counter-Print

"He is a genius. I think that many of his works are simply unbeatable."

3.
Logo for the Spanish railway system, Renfe.

—

4.
Spanish bank notes.

Cruz Novillo

"I have spent 60 years carrying out the same procedure: first think and then draw. Never draw without having the idea in the head, or in the heart."

To begin at the beginning. Tell us about your childhood in Spain. Who were some of the people that influenced you to pursue an artistic career?____ The first person I want to mention is the sculptor Fausto Culebras, who directed the Escuela de Artes y Oficios de Cuenca (the School of Arts and Crafts of Cuenca) when I was 15 years old. He is the first artist I ever met and he left an indelible mark on me, to the point that I knew that I wanted to dedicate myself to what he did, which seemed to me an enviable job. Since I was a child, I liked to take portraits of my school friends and family, and I always had the support of my parents.

How did you find the transition between being a student of fine art and your employment in the advertising agency Clarín?____ Really, I've never considered myself an art student. In the Escuela de Artes y Oficios de Cuenca we were dedicated to drawing statues with charcoal, blending tools and so on. I never even used colour in those exercises. Later on, during my student life at the Law School, I was left with very little free time, until I was lucky enough to be hired at a major advertising agency in Madrid. It was a great coincidence, as I found myself strolling through Madrid with a painter friend who worked in Publicidad Clarín and suggested that I accompany him to the agency. They gave me some test jobs, they liked my work and they hired me very quickly.

In 1965 you left Clarín to set up your own agency, did you have clients on board straight away?____ I started from scratch. When I left, I was already the art director of the agency and I had a very promising future, also from an economic point of view. On top of that, I had also just gotten married. I gave up that security, however, to create my own design studio together with my colleague Fernando Olmos, when designers were not even termed in such a way: we were cartoonists or graphic artists.

To my surprise, shortly after opening the studio, it was the Clarín agency that began calling me to carry out my work and three years later, I finally settled down alone, shortly before the birth of my first child, Pepe.

I can see your influence in many young designers today, who were your design heroes?____ Access to the media 60 years ago was very limited. I began to be interested very soon by the drafters who worked in the newspapers of Madrid, for example the drawings of Menéndez Chacón in the newspaper ABC. I have also admired Manolo Prieto. As for my international references, I began to know of them when I entered Clarín on November 9, 1958, thanks to the books and magazines that were available in our library, which showed me for the first time how design was created around the world. I still remember the impact that the Coca-Cola Corporate Identity Manual had on me when I saw it at the agency.

Can you tell us about your working process?____ Almost from the beginning, and until today, everything I've been drawing I've thought of before putting pencil to paper. Thought, reflection, ideas... are always prior to drawing. I have spent 60 years carrying out the same procedure: first think and then draw. Never draw without having the idea in the head, or in the heart. Therefore, I have never felt fear about a blank sheet.

Your logo designs are iconic, what are your thoughts on what makes a great logo?____ Let the ideas be powerful. I read long ago that the structuralism of French linguists handled three ideas: a semantic idea, a syntactic idea and a pragmatic idea. I applied it quickly to drawing and that is the process I follow. I strive to have a powerful semantic idea, I try to draw it in the best possible way (what I would call syntactic), then I review it so that it acquires a pragmatic quality—is it possible to reproduce that drawing by any technology, process, material, tool and so on? That is what I tried when I was a young man of 21 years and what I am still trying today. A sign must be significant. The biggest defect of a logo would be its insignificance.

What is the project you are most proud of?____ It depends on the season. These days, there is much talk in the media of the brand that I made in 1977 for the Spanish Socialist Party and it is a job that I still feel proud of 40 years later. In addition, the PSOE continues to use it exactly as I drew it. I also think my decision to design the uniforms of the Police in blue was highly relevant, replacing their earlier brown colour.

How do you stay inspired?____ I work a lot in the world of ideas. If I had not taken the habit of drawing, I would surely be a writer, for I would have been interested in converting my ideas into literature. I do not regret it, because I have had a good time dedicating myself to the world of sensory perception.

I am also inspired by reading texts on quantum physics, which I have long been fond of. And above all, I read poetry.

What has been your most challenging project?____ Any creation of corporate identity which required identity guidelines. It is always this that has given me the most work—think of the standardisation systems for the implementation of a brand. It has always been easier for me to create the signs of those marks.

You have had a lasting career as a designer, how has the industry changed in this time?____ At every moment, the design industry has been making huge leaps. The last of them, which took us to the digitised world, has been the most important of all, to the point that I do not believe that in the future the industry will

produce such a radical change again. However, I do not think that the improvement of the tools necessarily implies an improvement in the quality of the works, neither in design nor in any other creative activity.

> **"The designer is an archer who shoots the arrow in order to hit the center of the target. The artist is an archer who shoots the arrow and, in the place where it has been nailed, paints the target."**

You also work as a sculptor, as well as a graphic designer. How does this art form inform your graphic design work?____ They 100% reciprocally influence each other. I think I have reached a point where the border between the two worlds has disappeared for me. Art and design are different things, but exercised in my case by the same person. Many years ago I came up with this phrase, 'the designer is an archer who shoots the arrow in order to hit the center of the target. The artist is an archer who shoots the arrow and, in the place where it has been nailed, paints the target'. In my work as a sculptor, I use the vast knowledge that I have acquired as a designer, and vice versa. The naturalness with which I accept this, in this phase of my life, is amazing.

What is the best piece of advice you could give to designers starting out today?____ Do not ever copy. Nothing. Designing is creating.

Would you do anything differently if you could start all over again?____ From the professional point of view, definitely not. I would still think that in order to make marks, it is best to take a compass and a pencil, not a pot of paint and a brush, which was what I found on my desk the first day of my professional life.

Building

Navarro y Navarro

Construction company. 1968.

Urbis

Construction company. 1975.

Pacsa

Construction company. 1992.

Pacsa exterior
graphics.

Construcciones y Contratas

Construction company. 1988.

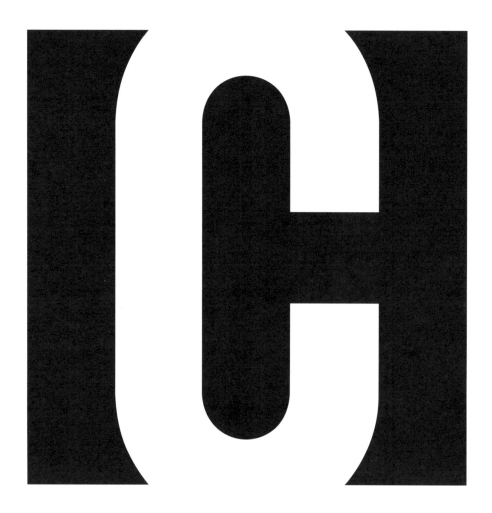

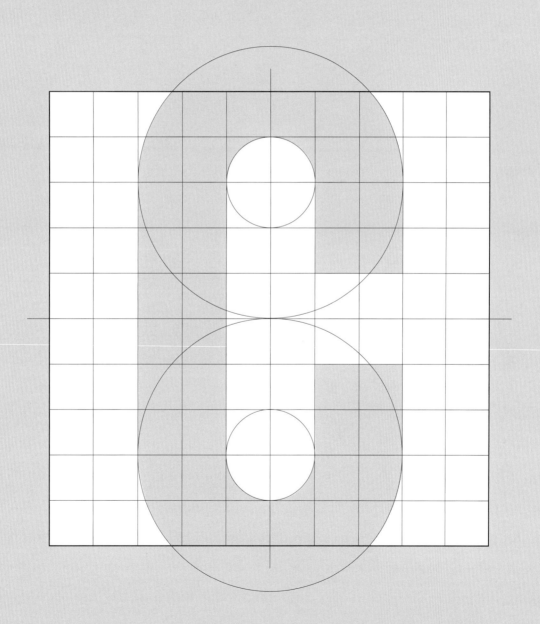

Focycsa

Fomento de Construcciones y Contratas. Construction company. 1991.

Estrella 6

Construction company. 1968.

Huarte

Construction company. 1967.

Construcciones Nertal

Construction company. 1966.

Corporate gift for
Entrecanales y Távora.

Entrecanales y Távora

Construction company. 1973.

Creative Director: Fernando Olmos.

Premio Agustín de Betancourt

International infrastructure awards organised by Colegio de Ingenieros de Caminos, Canales y Puertos. 2015.

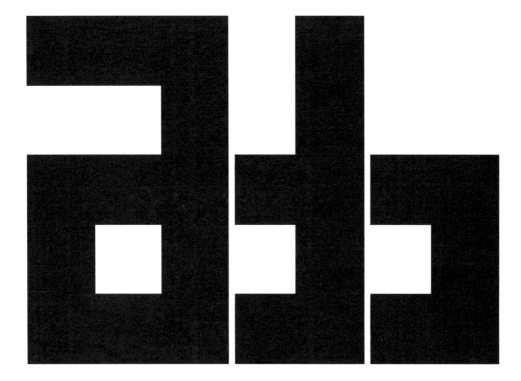

Creative Director: Pepe Cruz.

Sculpture for Premio
Agustín de Betancourt.

Premio Leopoldo Calvo Sotelo

Public leadership award organised by Colegio de Ingenieros de Caminos, Canales y Puertos. 2016.

Creative Director: Pepe Cruz.

Instituto de Promoción Pública de la Vivienda

Institute of housing public promotion. Ministry of Housing. 1976.

Premio Rafael Izquierdo a la Solidaridad

Solidarity award organised by Colegio de Ingenieros de Caminos, Canales y Puertos. 2014.

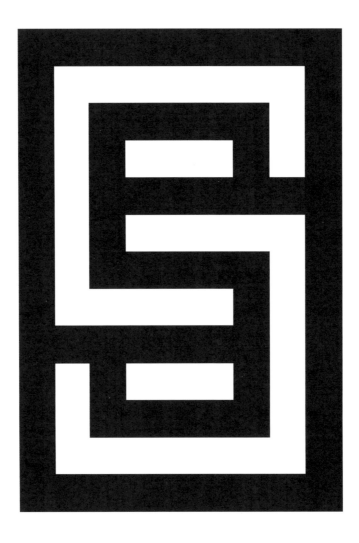

Creative Director: Pepe Cruz.

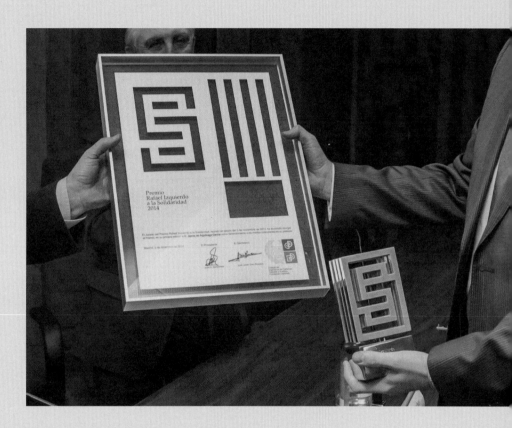

Sculpture & framed award
for Premio Rafael Izquierdo
a la Solidaridad.

Exterior artwork.

Cement bag.

PORTLAND VALDERRIVAS

In 1981 Cruz Novillo created the visual identity of this Spanish company, dedicated to the production of cement and other materials for construction.

The logo, which is still used by the company, consists of three superimposed triangles. For over ten years, the corporate colour was red, but was replaced in 1993 by the colour green, to show the greater environmental involvement of the corporation.

In addition, Portland Valderrivas, as co-owner of the Torre Picasso building in Madrid, commissioned Cruz Novillo to create various sculptures and works of signage for the building, including for its parking. For this work, Cruz Novillo employed a system of numbers and colours that indicated the floor and the parking section. The colour code, which uses green, blue, orange and yellow, changes on each of the four floors, using the ramp helix as a connection, generating an attractive and surprising solution.

Torre Picasso parking signage.

Portland Valderrivas

Cement company. 1981.

Grupo Uralita

Building materials. 1993.

Provialsa

Promotora de viviendas de Alcudia. Housing promoter. 1973.

Metropolitan

Real estate company. 2000.

Creative Director: Pepe Cruz.

Per Inmobiliaria

Real estate company. 1987.

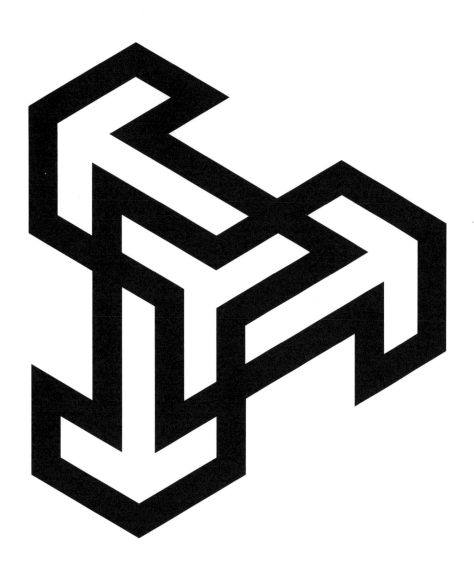

Grupo Velázquez

Real estate group. 1981.

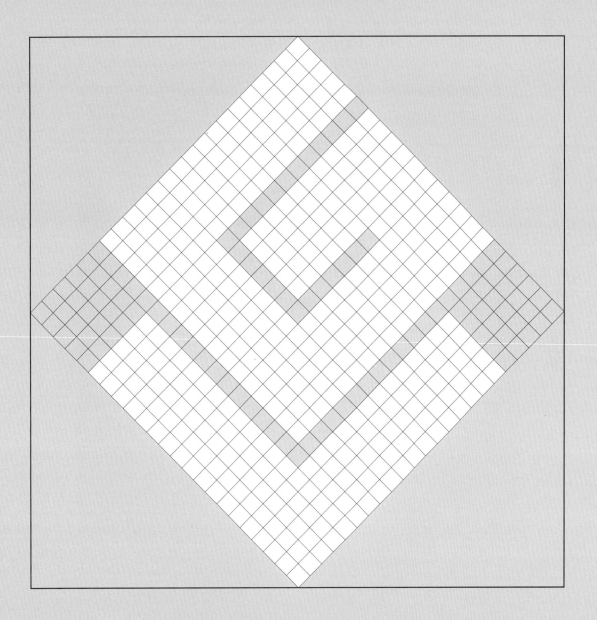

Inmobiliaria Metrovacesa

Real estate company. 1973.

Inmobiliaria Espronceda

Real estate company. 1973.

Inmobiliaria Galdácano

Real estate company. 1973.

Inmobiliaria Pérez Román

Real estate company. 1973.

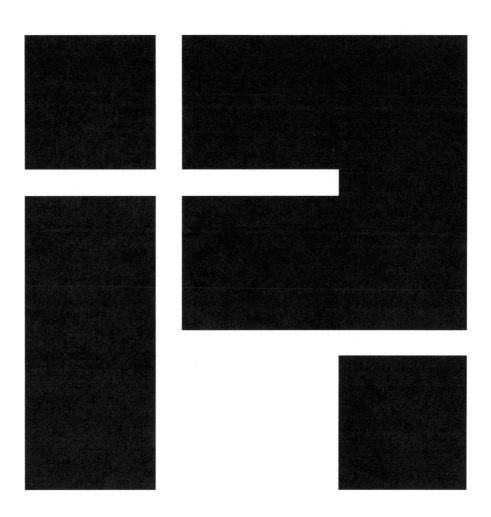

Inmobiliaria Ural

Real estate company. 1973.

Inmobiliaria Vasco-Holandesa

Real estate company. 1973.

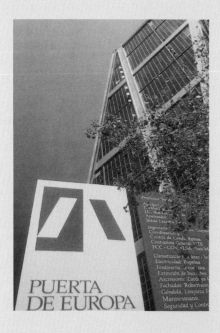

Exterior signage.

Sculptures for
Puerta de Europa.

Exterior art work.

Twin leaning towers in Madrid. 1994.

Premio Acueducto de Segovia

Engineering prize. Colegio de Ingenieros de Caminos, Canales y Puertos. 2014.

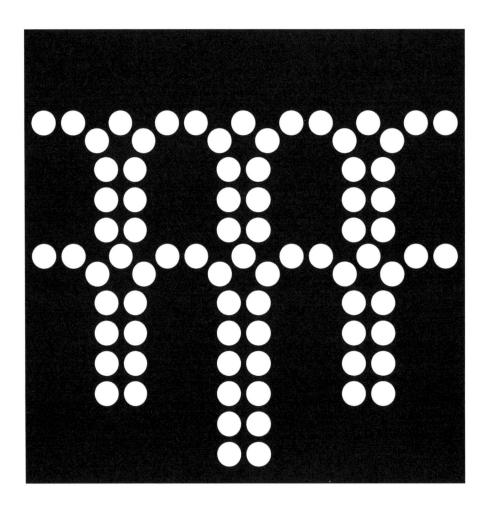

Creative Director: Pepe Cruz.

Oliveros

Group of buildings in Almería by architect Ángel Jaramillo. 1979.

La Berzosa

Urbanisation in Madrid. 1976.

Atlantis

Urbanisation in Roquetas de Mar. 1976.

Playa Serena

Urbanisation in Almeria. 1975.

El Pinar

Urbanisation in Madrid. 1973.

Business

Cruz Novillo — Logos

Pool

Group of service companies. 1979.

Dipresa

Professional association of agricultural enterprises. 1995.

Corporacion 25

Business companies. 1977.

Dopp Consulting

Department of psycho-professional orientation. 1966.

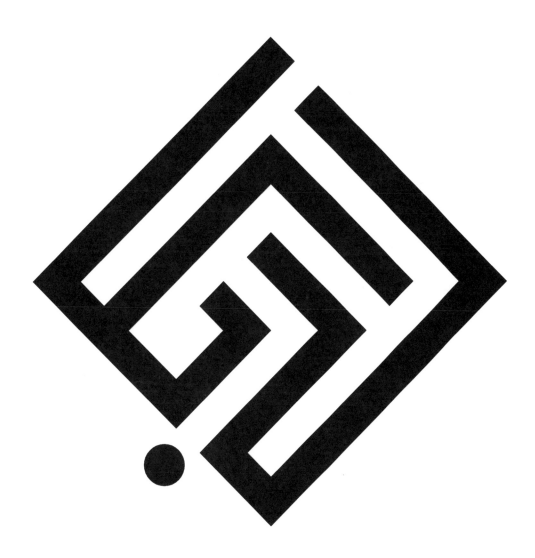

Creative Director: Fernando Olmos.

Ibercobre

Copper company. 1979.

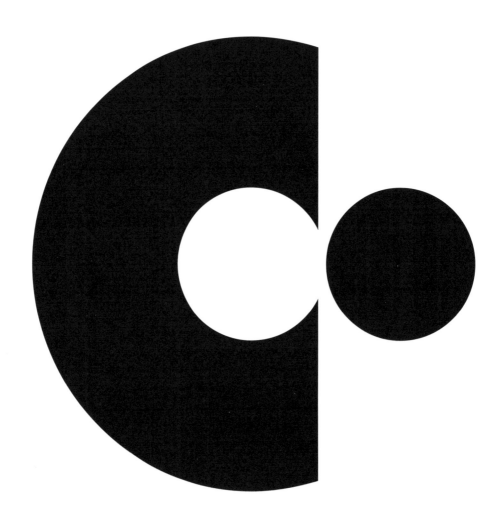

Ibercobre multiple
sculpture in bronze
& copper.

Zamorano

Hairdresser. 1970.

Laboratorios Alter

Illustration for pharmaceutical laboratories. 1973.

Trebol

International trading. 1984.

Bolin

Pen factory. 1964.

Consultores de Comunicación y Dirección

Communication & management consultants. 1988.

Village haberdashery. 1957.

Ifsa

International franchising. 1984.

Diverplay

Toy distributor. 1982.

Bosca

Service company. 1983.

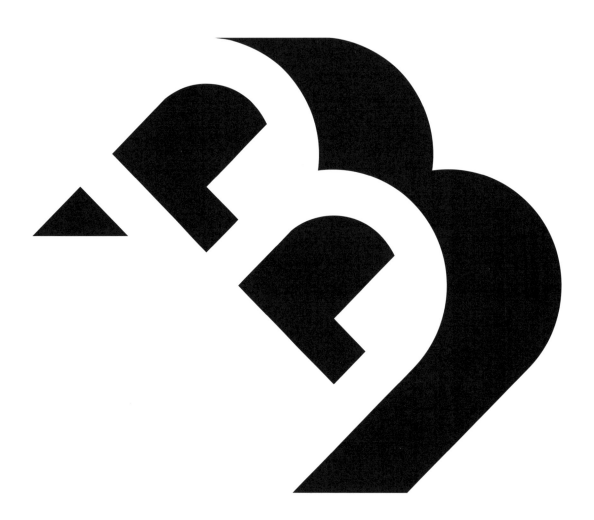

Culture & Art

Cruz Novillo — Logos

Portal

Art gallery. 1970.

Galeria Peninsula

Art gallery. 1973.

Marta Moriarty

Art. 2017.

Creative Director: Pepe Cruz.

Art gallery. 1987.

Madart

Art gallery. 1998.

Creative Director: Pepe Cruz.

Museo Español de Arte Contemporáneo

Spanish contemporary art museum. 1968.

Toscar

Art gallery. 1969.

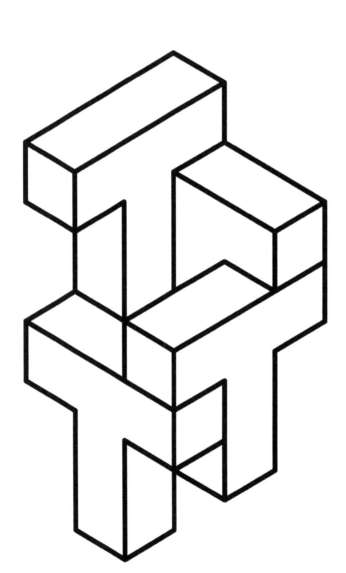

Fademesa

Metal foundry for sculptors. 1986.

Mundiarte

Editor of works of art. 1981.

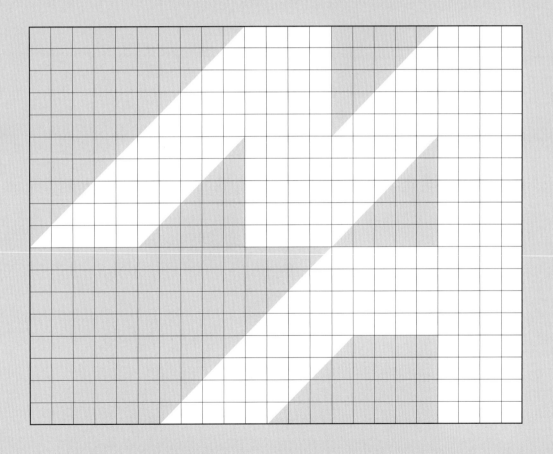

Arcadio Blasco

Sculptor. 2010.

Vacae XX Anniversary

Artist group (Alfonso Albacete, Concha Alvaro, Dominique Bernis, Cruz Novillo, Titto Ferreira, Julio Peñas, Cristina Rodríguez Vela, Jacobo Pérez Enciso, Alberto Campo Baeza & Roberto Turégano). 2013.

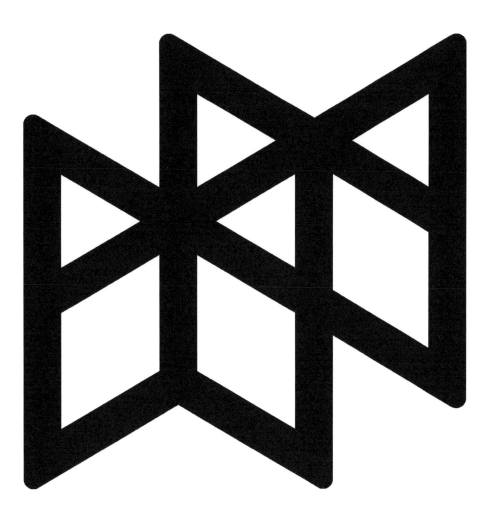

Fundación Pilar Citoler

Art foundation. Cycle of 32 unique & different sculptures. 2014.

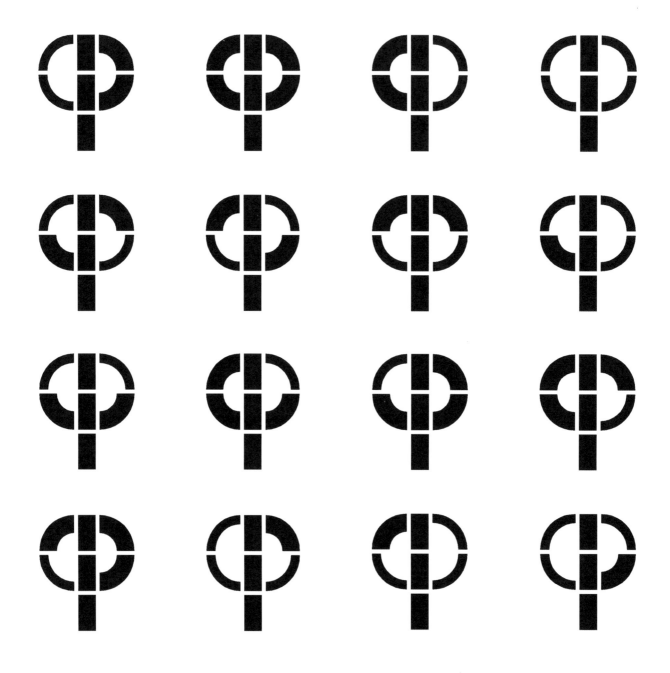

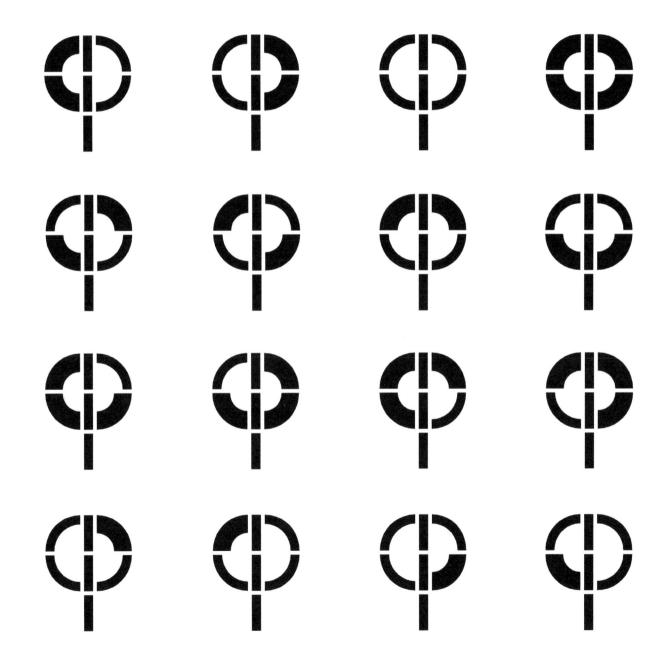

Anselmo Alvarez

Art gallery. 1989.

Architecture studio. 1970.

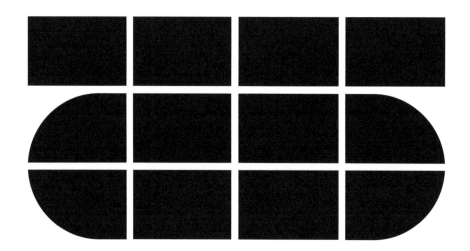

Architect. 1971.

Unión Internacional de Arquitectos

Architects International Union. 1974.

Moreno Barberá

Architect. 1970.

Apetai

Association of architecture & interiors. 1998.

Congreso de la Union Internacional de Arquitectos

Congress of the International Union of Architects. 1974.

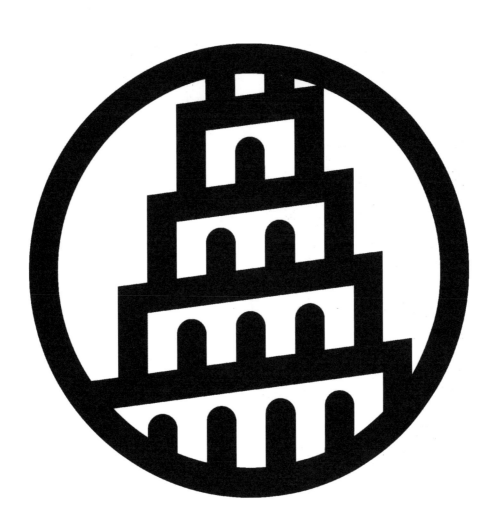

90.

feliz Navidad y próspero año 1972

Arquinde

Greetings card
for Arquinde.

Architecture & engineering. 1969.

Fundacion Antonio Camuñas

Architecture foundation. 1989.

Multiple stainless steel
sculpture for Fundacion
Antonio Camuñas.

Urbanismo Español en America

Spanish urbanism in America exhibition. 1974.

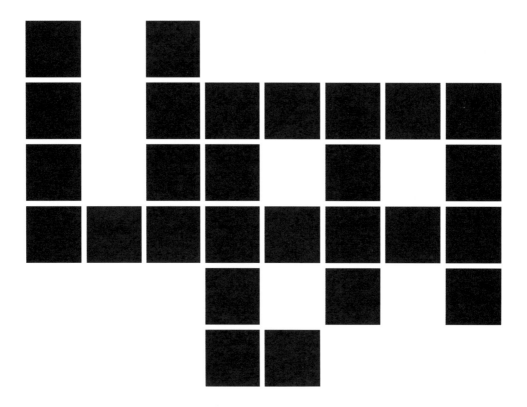

Luis Megino

Film producer. 1982.

Creative Director: Eugenia Alcorta.

CineCorto

Short film production company. 1960.

Cinepaq

Film distributors. 1989.

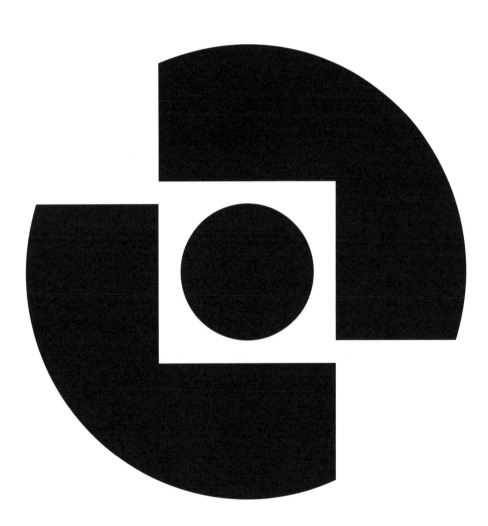

Elías Querejeta

Cinema producer. 1989.

Promotion of cinema rooms. 1990.

Film producer. 1982.

Cines Luna

Four cinemas in Madrid. 1979.
Full moon, waning crescent, fourth quarter & new moon.

Festival de Cine Iberoamericano de Huelva

Film festival. 1974.

Círculo de Bellas Artes

Cultural institution. 1968

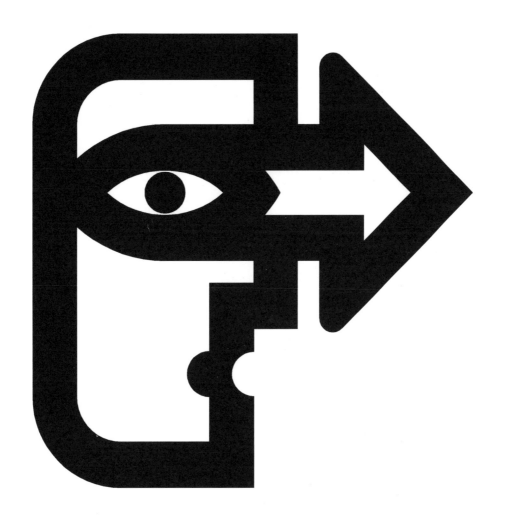

Premio Planeta de Fotografía

Planeta photography prize. 1981.

Auditorio Manuel de Falla

Auditorium. 1982.

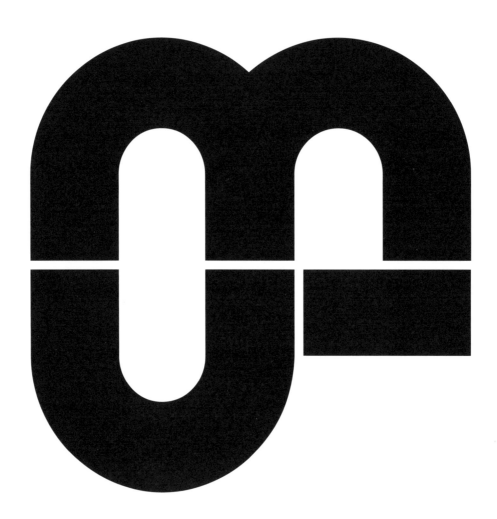

Feria de Artesanía

Madrid craft fair. 1994.

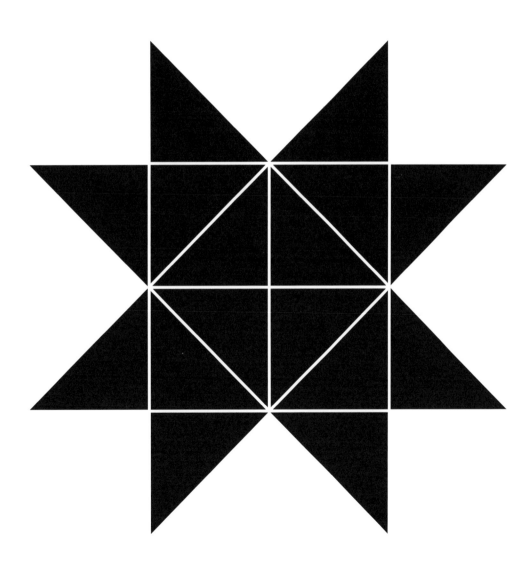

Crisis

Disco. 1984.

Theos

Disco. 1975.

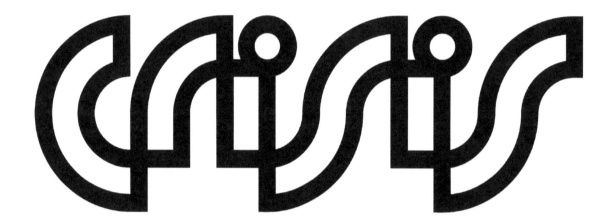

Música Antigua Aranjuez

Antique music festival. 1994.

Centro Nacional de Exposiciones

National Exhibitions Centre. Ministry of Culture. 1993.

Festival de Jazz

Madrid jazz festival. 1993.

Madrid jazz festival. 1993.

Festival de Jazz

Madrid jazz festival. 1993.

European White Nights, cultural event. 2007.

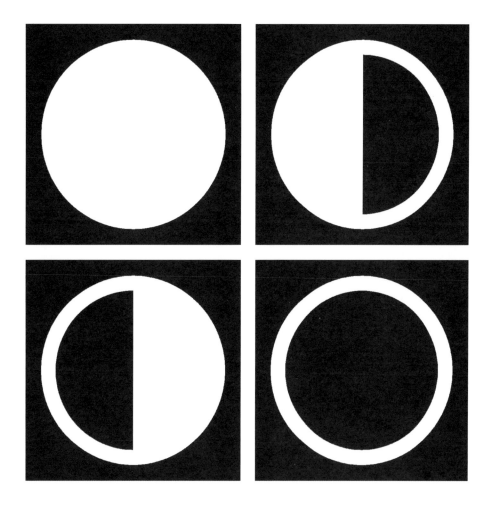

Creative Director: Pepe Cruz.

Bicentenario de los Estados Unidos de America

Bicentennial of the USA. 1975.

Sticker designs for the
Bicentenario de los
Estados Unidos de
America.

Spanish Government Commemorations

1808 2008 Bicentennial of the War of Independence
1808 1814 Exhibition: Spain, the Nation in War
1810 2010 Bicentennial of the independence of the Ibero-American republics
1812 2012 Bicentennial of the proclamation of the Constitution of Cádiz

Creative Director: Pepe Cruz.

Escala

Decoration studio. 1972.

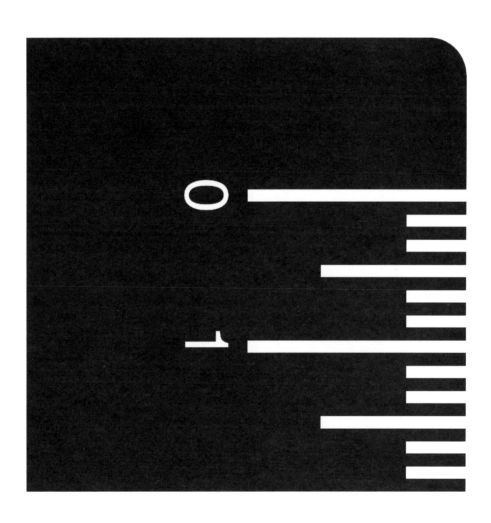

Quinto Centenario del Descubrimiento de America

500th anniversary of the discovery of America. 1981.

Event merchandising for
the 500th anniversary of
the discovery of America.

Lugares de La Mancha

Exhibition. 1970.

Diseño en Cuenca

Design in Cuenca. 1998.

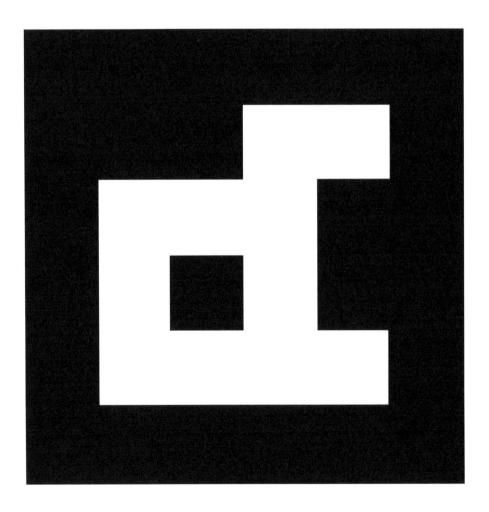

Cultural event in Cuenca. 1987.

Cuenca 2016

Commemoration of world heritage city by Unesco. 2015.
823.543 different logos (all the possible combinations of the seven colours and musical notes).

1.
Signage for
Cuenca 2016.
—
2.
Printed materials.
—
3.
Sculpture.

4.
Cuenca 2016 art
exhibition poster,
which is also the music
sheet of a 7 minute
and 21 second piano
concert in seven
movements: Red (Do),
Orange (Re), Yellow
(Mi), Green (Fa),
Blue (Sol), Grey (La)
& Magenta (Si).

Tilde

Theatre group. 1986.

Martin Merlo

Taylor. 1999.

Creative Director: Pepe Cruz.

Angeles Andany

Fashion designer. 1974.

De Natura

Craft factory & showroom of the designer Paco Muñoz. 1971.

Berceli

Kitchen furniture. 2008.

Creative Director: Pepe Cruz.

Calpernia

Design editions by Antonio Serrano & Mar López. 1995.

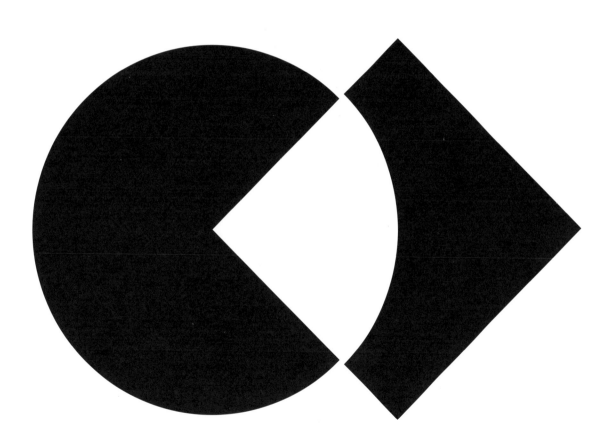

Fundación Antonio Machado

Socialist Party poetry foundation. 1976.

Ameda

Asociación de Mueblistas Españoles de Diseño Actual. Furniture. 1968.

Kemen

Office furniture. 1974.

Kemen showroom
exterior signage.

Internal signage.

Signes

Manufacturing and implementation of corporate identity and signage by Lluis Morón
& Carmen Revilla. 1997.

hache muebles

Furniture. 1969.

Temas de Diseño

Bimonthly industrial design magazine. 1972.

Clarín

Advertising agency. 1964.

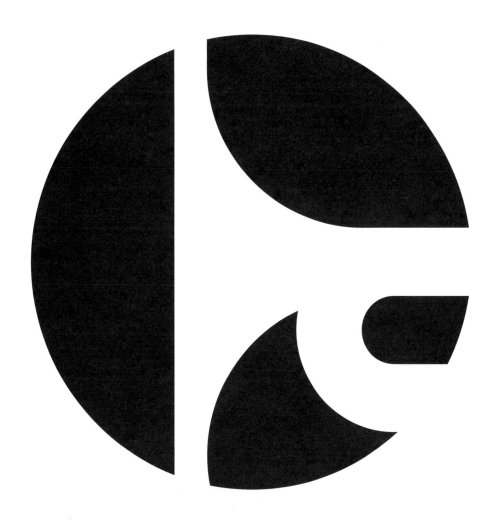

Signos del Siglo

100 years of graphic design in Spain exhibition. 1999.

DdA

Events design. 1995.

Creative Director: Miryam Anllo.

Christmas greeting
card design for DdA.

Cruz más Cruz

Design studio. 2007.

CRUZ MÁS CRUZ

As they define themselves, Cruz más Cruz is a design, architecture and art studio based in Madrid, founded by Cruz Novillo (designer and sculptor) and his son Pepe Cruz (designer and architect) who believe that it is possible to improve the environment through art and design, trying to innovate in each of their works.

Both the name and the design of the company's visual identity were created by Cruz Novillo and his son Pepe, who generated an attractive and ingenious solution that has the conceptual weight that permeates all of Cruz Novillo's work. The key is that the surname 'Cruz' and the word 'more' share a symbol, which generates a sign that, when used in 12 corporate colours (referring to the work 'Diafragma dodecafónico' by Cruz Novillo), can be combined in the company's corporate stationery in millions (8.916.100.448.256) of ways.

In addition to the everyday activity of the studio and subject to the design and architectural commissions and the exhibitions of Cruz Novillo as an artist, in recent years they have been attending numerous events together as lecturers, including, amongst many others, the 2013 Blanc Festival in the Catalan town of Vilanova i la Geltrú and MAD in Spain (Madrid) in 2014.

Since the beginning of 2015, they have offered an online course called 'Bi-dimensional and Three-dimensional Corporate Identity', which already has more than 1000 students on the Domestika design website, confirming that the work of Cruz Novillo continues to raise interest 60 years after beginning his career at the advertising agency Clarín, in 1958.

Stationery design for Cruz más Cruz.

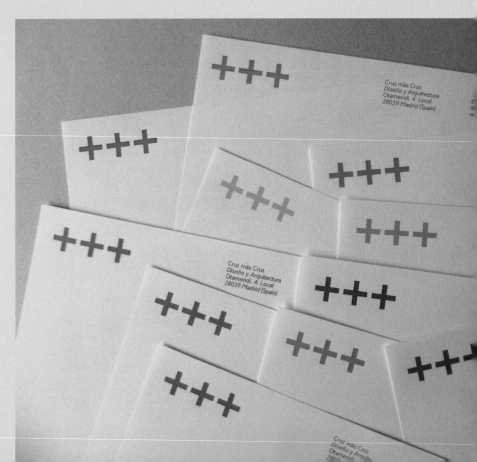

Cruz más Cruz

2011 New year greeting. 1+1×10×10×10+10+1=2011 (the logo of Cruz más Cruz consisting of '+++'). 2010.

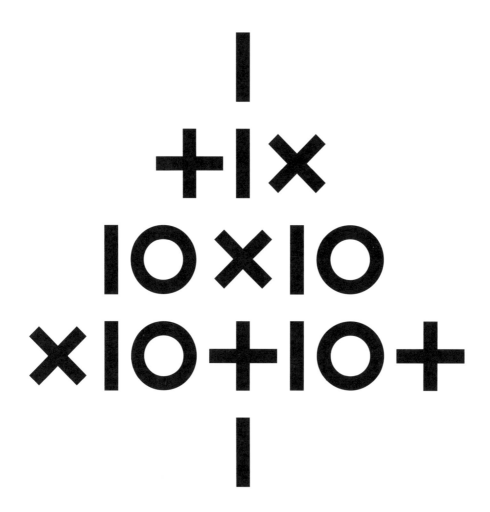

Creative Director: Pepe Cruz.

Education

Cruz Novillo — Logos

Colegio San Fernando

School. 1975.

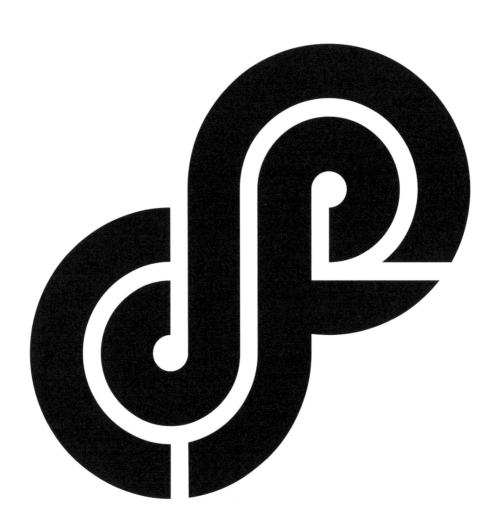

Best

Language courses in England. 1988.

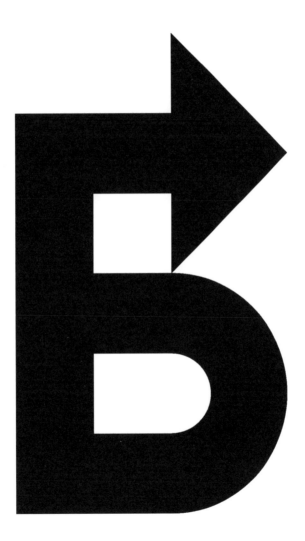

Creative Director: Pepe Cruz.

Colegio de Ingenieros de Caminos, Canales y Puertos

College of Civil Engineers. 2012.

In cooperation with Estudio Turégano. Creative Director: Pepe Cruz.

Sculpture for Colegio de
Ingenieros de Caminos,
Canales y Puertos.

153.

Professional merit medal.

COLEGIO DE INGENIEROS DE CAMINOS, CANALES Y PUERTOS

———

In 2012 Cruz más Cruz, in collaboration with Estudio Turégano, won a restricted competition for the creation of the new visual identity for the College of Civil Engineers.

The project, to a large extent, consisted of signage, publishing, digital applications and three-dimensional works, such as sculptures, badges and medals.

In the signage works for the headquarters of the college in Madrid, Cruz más Cruz created a modular system that adapts to the wide variety of fittings presented by the set of buildings, collaborating again with the Barcelona company Signes, specialists in the implementation of visual identity systems.

It is interesting to observe together the family of marks created for the Colegio de Caminos, the Caminos Foundation and the House of Engineering, with their combination of rectangular and semicircular shapes, each with a clearly sculptural (three-dimensional) feeling.

This journey back and forth between the two and three dimensions is also evident in other works for the same client, such as the Medals of Honour, the Acueducto de Segovia Prize, the Leopoldo Calvo-Sotelo Prize and the Agustín de Betancourt Prize, which presents an interesting revision of the concept of a 'diploma', which was stripped of any classicism.

Cruz Novillo created multiple signed and numbered sculptures in polished aluminum, which are available in the shop of the Colegio de Ingenieros and a large format sculpture (3×3×2m) for the patio accessing the building.

Casa de la Ingeniería. Colegio de Ingenieros de Caminos, Canales y Puertos

College of Civil Engineers. House of Engineering. 2012.

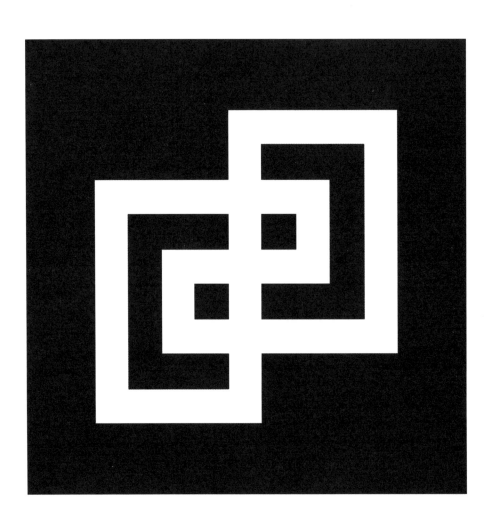

Fundación Caminos. Colegio de Ingenieros de Caminos, Canales y Puertos

College of Civil Engineers. Foundation. 2012.

Universidad Francisco de Vitoria

University in Madrid. 2012.

Creative Director: Pepe Cruz.

UNIVERSIDAD FRANCISCO DE VITORIA

Both Cruz Novillo and Pepe Cruz have been professors in design, fine arts and architecture at the Universidad Francisco de Vitoria (Madrid) since 2010. In 2012, they were commissioned by the rector Daniel Sada to redesign the university's own corporate identity, with the request not to make drastic changes and with respect to what had been used so far. For this reason, they decided to take advantage of the graphical and symbolic potential of the previous symbol but to introduce a substantial change: they rotated each of the four sharp forms 180° and redrew them with rounded tips, eliminating the symbol's aggressiveness. In doing so, they made the negative space penetrate into the interior of the symbol, moving the positive space to the perimeter and facilitating its reproduction at very small sizes.

As for the colour range, the dark blue colour was maintained and the previous Optima typography was replaced by the Helvetica family, an absolute design classic with a modernity that was considered ideal for this project. Cruz Novillo is currently working on a series of small format sculptures and a large sculpture in steel for the campus of the University in Pozuelo de Alarcón (Madrid).

Sculpture for Universidad Francisco de Vitoria.

Museo de Ciencia y Tecnología

Museum of science & technology. 1980.

Fundación Esfuerzo Solidario

Solidarity Effort Foundation. United Firemen Without Borders (donated work). 2010.

Creative Director: Pepe Cruz.

Consejo Superior de Colegios de Farmaceuticos

Superior Council of Colleges of Pharmacists. 1969.

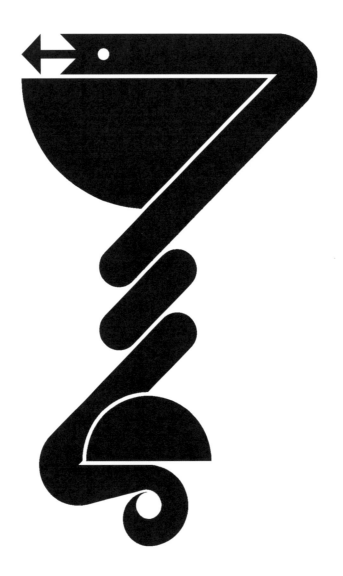

Energy

Cruz Novillo – Logos

Endesa

National Spanish electricity. 1988.

ENDESA

In 1988 Endesa (Empresa Nacional de Electricidad), launched a large media campaign where it presented the new visual identity of the company.

The new symbol, of blunted angles, uses the form of a ray to reference the symbology that the firm had used in recent years. It was also designed to be used by all the Group's companies (Endesa, Encasur, Enher, Gesa, ERZ and Unelco), thus representing its unity within the electricity sector.

For the main identity the colour palette is a combination of grey and blue and a sans serif typeface is used to accompany it.

In 1993, on the occasion of the 50th anniversary of the company, Cruz Novillo created a symbol in which he again used the symbolism of the ray, this time inscribed in a circle and with a typographic approach specifically created for this project.

Sculpture for Endesa.

Endesa 50 Aniversario
embroidered logo
& keyring.

Endesa 50 Aniversario

National Spanish electricity 50th anniversary. 1993.

Crespo y Blasco

Electrical installations. 1978.

Heating manufacturers. 1972.

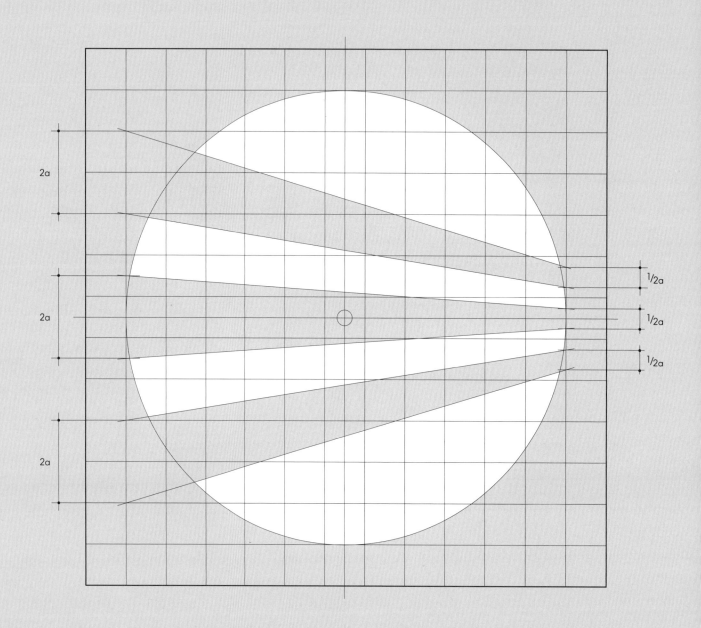

2a

2a

2a

2a

1/2a

1/2a

1/2a

Red Eléctrica

National distribution of electricity. 1987.

Repsol

Oil company. 1996.

REPSOL

In 1995 Cruz Novillo received an extensive commission from Repsol, the first Spanish oil company, including the design of a visual identity system and corporate stationery, the creation of a dozen standards manuals, various sculptures and a collaboration in designing spaces and products with architects Juan Eizaguirre and Norman Foster. This was a project in which the figure of the engineer Alfonso Cortina, then Repsol president, was fundamental.

Although Cruz Novillo was completely creatively free to work, he decided to respect the historical identity of Repsol and proposed a profound update of the brand created by Wolff Olins in 1986. Cruz Novillo retained the colour palette of orange, red and a blue horizon but simplified the forms, gave greater symmetry and readjusted the typography.

Cruz Novillo collaborated with Norman Foster on the service stations; large 'mushrooms' with a central mast which, with varying heights, are overlapping and covering the fuel pumps. Its white, orange and red colours are complemented by the dark blue walls of the central building, where the payment office and shop are located. This decision, taken by the designer, made the application of the Repsol brand on the architecture itself unnecessary. The application in the monolith was also innovative, where the logotype is vertical and reads from bottom to top.

In addition, as a sculptor, Cruz Novillo made two large-format sculptures: 'Doble sol contrapuesto' (2×2.52×3.58m) made of corten steel for the company's headquarters, and 'Doble sol contrapuesto vaciado', which was four times larger than the previous one and made from stainless steel for the Repsol Technology Center located in Móstoles.

1.
256 unique Repsol sculptures
in methacrylate & aluminum.
—
2.
Repsol multiple sculpture
in bronze & steel.
—
3.
Petrol station forecourt.
Architect: Norman Foster.

Repsol gasoline
tank in Vigo.

Repsol stainless
steel sculpture
in Móstoles.

Oil tanker & forecourt.

Inisolar

Renewable energy. 1980.

Savitra

Renewable energy. 2007.

Creative Director: Pepe Cruz.

Instituto Tecnológico Geominero de España

Geological & mining institute. 1988.

Engineering & Industry

Cruz Novillo – Logos

Tecnigesa

Engineering company. 1971.

Engineering. 1984.

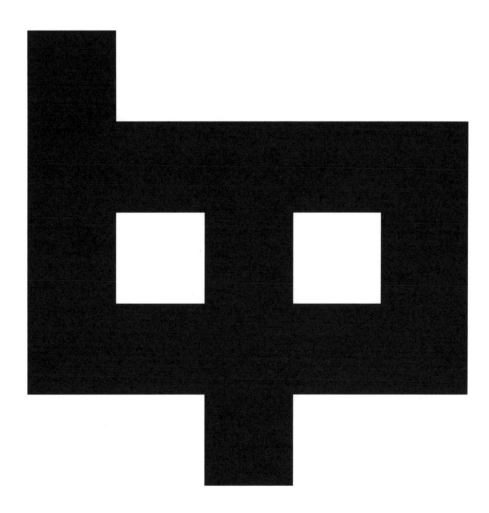

Ofirex

Industrial machinery. 1987.

Industrias Aragonesas

Industrial corporation. 1972.

Monacril

Chemical industry. 1972.

Finance

Cruz Novillo – Logos

Caja de Ahorros de Sevilla. El Monte

Bank. 1988.

Banco Cooperativo

Bank. 1990.

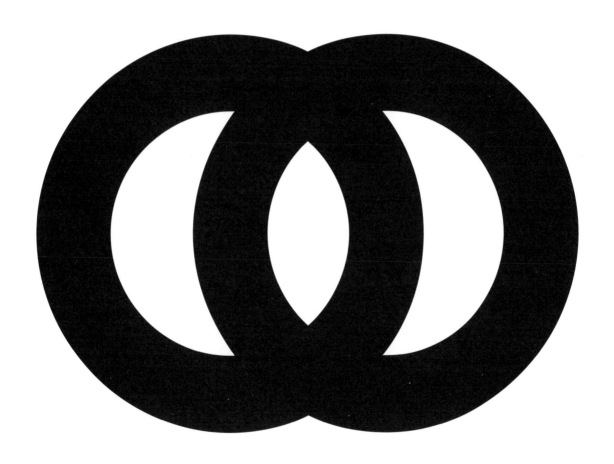

Banco Pastor

Bank. 1988.

Bancal

Agricultural credit bank. 1971.

Banco Exterior de España

Illustration for a bank. 1979.

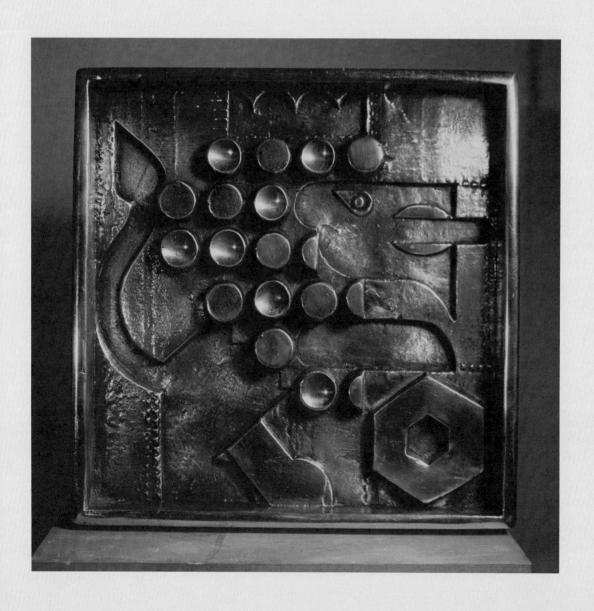

Banco Industrial de Leon

Industrial bank of Leon. 1972.

Banco de Fomento

Bank. 1973.

Banco Zaragozano

Bank. 1989.

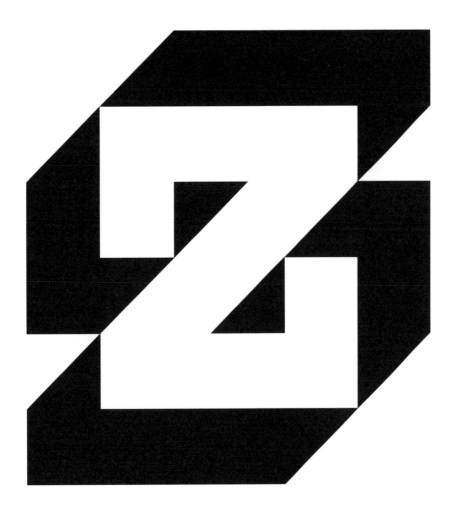

Induban

Industrial financing bank. 1972.

El Monte. Caja de Ahorros de Sevilla

Bank. 1989.

Banco de Vizcaya multiple sculpture
in bronze & stone.

Exterior stainless steel sculpture
in Madrid.

Exterior stainless steel sculpture
in Madrid.

Bank. 1975.

Banco del Comercio

Bank. 1989.

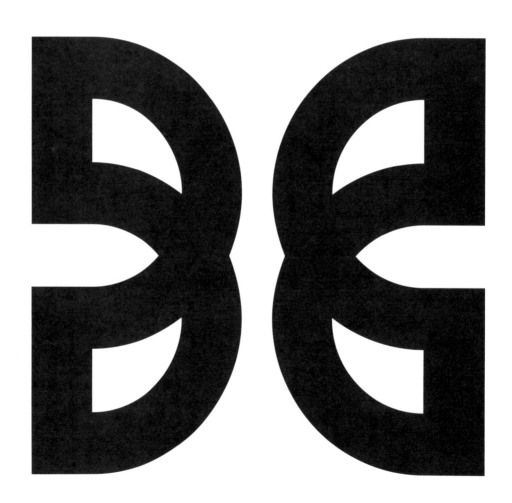

Meeting of the International Monetary Fund. 1993.

Safe

Money transfers. 2002.

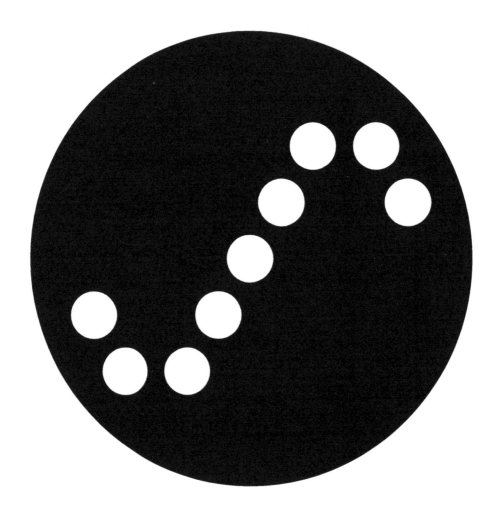

Creative Director: Pepe Cruz.

Giropais

National money transfers. 2011.

Creative Director: Pepe Cruz.

Incredit

Credit institute. 1979.

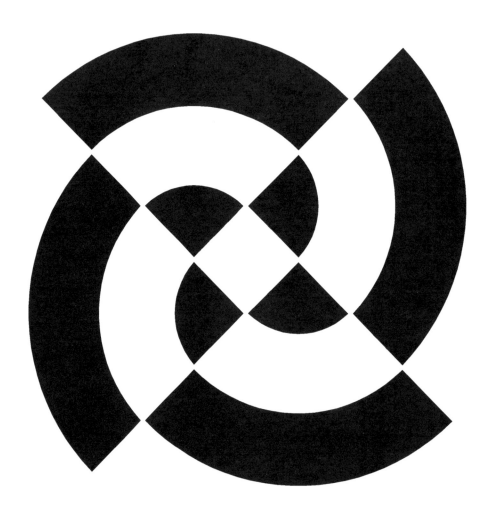

Finasa

Financial group. 1971.

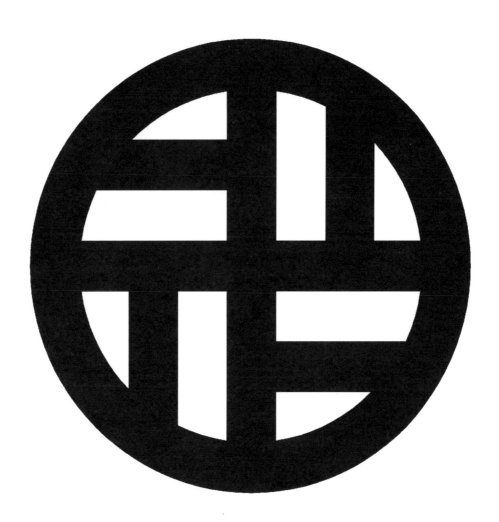

Tesoro Público

Spanish Public Treasury. 1984.

TESORO PÚBLICO

In 1983, the Government of Spain's Ministry of Economy entrusted Cruz Novillo with the visual identity for the Public Treasury and its associated products: state bonds, de-taxable debt, treasury bills, state obligations and treasury notes. Cruz Novillo was thus asked to bring into existence products that did not exist visually prior to his involvement.

The designer created for this client a symbol for each division of the Public Treasury, each composed of its initial and applied in different colours (brown, green, blue, red, orange and yellow). Each of the letters, a capital, has a crown on top.

All the graphics are composed of small circles that try to represent the economic activity carried out by the institution. For the logo, the typeface Lubalin Graph Medium is used, an Egyptian style of family created by the American designer Herb Lubalin, who Cruz Novillo had the opportunity to meet in New York in the early 60s.

During the 80s and 90s, Tesoro Público carried out numerous television campaigns, where the entire family of brands was used with a three-dimensional digital animation.

Tesoro Público corporate identity manual & company literarure.

Light

Financial services. 1978.

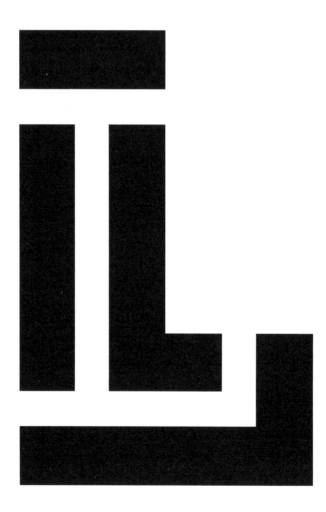

Icex

Spanish institute of foreign trade. 1998.

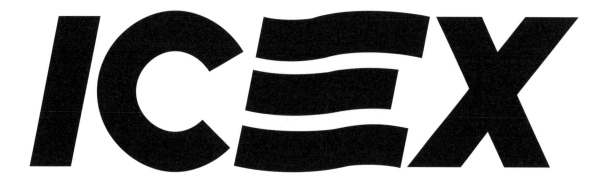

Sociedad de Tasación

Real estate valuation firm. 1984.

Food & Retail

Cruz Novillo — Logos

Actus

Bikini shop. 1979.

La Sirena

Supermarket in Almería. 1971.

Top Top

Fashion shop. 1982.

Pink

Fashion shop. 1983.

Creative Director: Amelia Jiménez.

Madrid Dos

Shopping centre. 1982.

Don Quijote & Sancho Panza merchandising campaign. 2008.

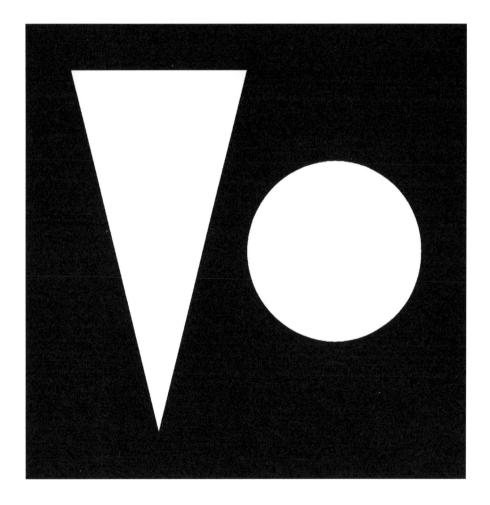

Creative Director: Pepe Cruz.

Menu de España

Spanish gastronomy promotion. 1992.

Sésamo

Cocktail-bar in a cave. 1982.

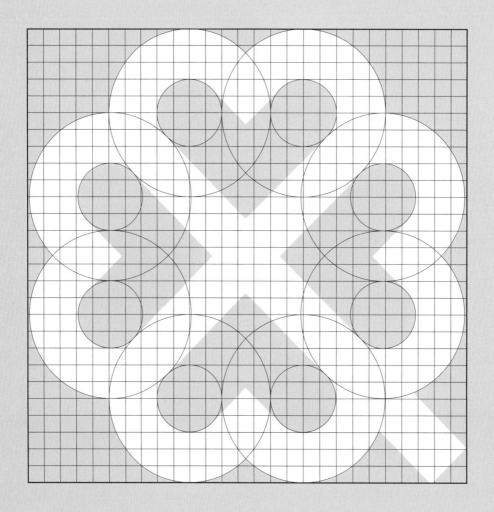

Somosierra

Ice cream manufacturer. 1990.

Font Romeu

Bar in Madrid. 1971.

Ruperto de Nola

Restaurant in the Torres Blancas building in Madrid. 1971.

Architect: Sáenz de Oiza. Interior architect: Luis Corbella.

Trapa

Chocolate manufacturer. 1985.

Vallegarcía

Winery. 2002.

Alfonso Cortina

Livestock farm. 1994.

Healthcare

Cruz Novillo — Logos

VISIONLAB

The symbol for Visionlab consists of the merger between an eye and a letter 'V', with the aim of being easily associated with the activity of the company and trying to achieve a balanced, powerful and enduring brand. This eye has been the leading signifier of the identity, being present in a great quantity of applications; from the glasses themselves to the packaging, the corporate stationery, the fleet of vehicles, the interior design of the shops and so on.

The logo was composed with Futura Medium, a typeface without serifs, which was made with small modifications in its form, especially the initial 'V', which is configured as an equilateral triangle and spaced to give it a distinctive feature. As an auxiliary typeface, Times was chosen, with a more classic cut. As for the colour palette, the main colour is dark red, which is accompanied by light red and occasionally orange and gold. It is a brand that the company continues to use almost 30 years after its creation, with hardly any modifications.

Visionlab

Optical laboratories. 1989.

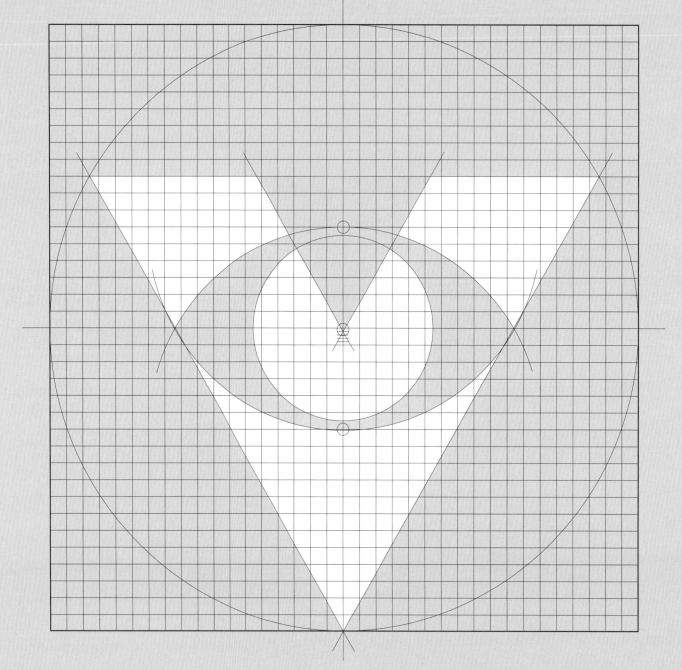

Instituto Ibys

Pharmaceutical group. 1968.

Sculpture for Expo Óptica.

International optics fair. 1984.

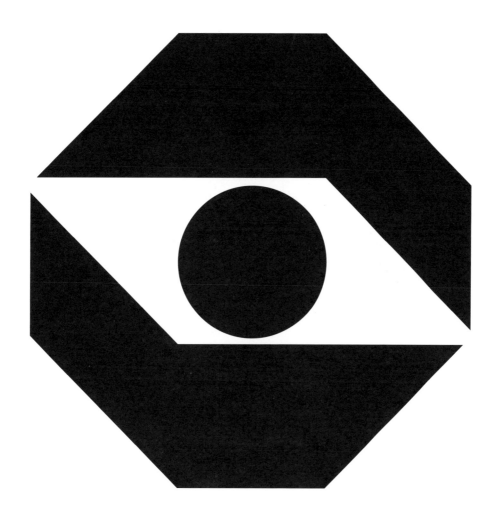

Product & packaging
design for Tridental.
(Model)

Tridental

Interdental cleaner. 2010.

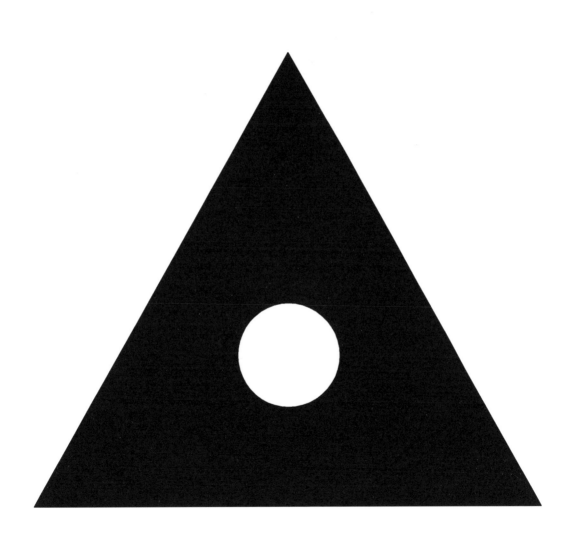

Indas

Pharmaceutical products. 1993.

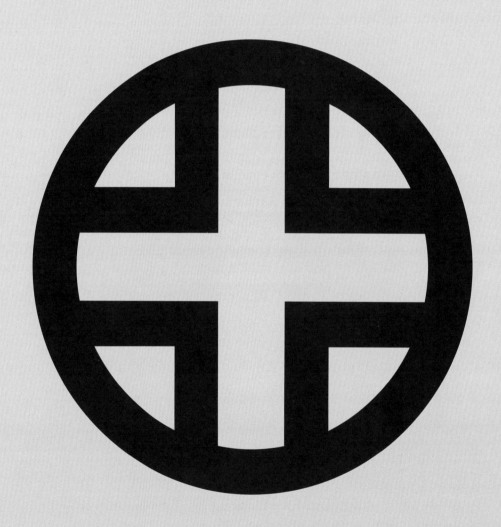

INDAS

Indas, which is an acronym for 'Industria del Algodón Sanitario', was founded in 1950 as a family business and sells hospital and hygiene products. During the following decades, the company continued to develop until consolidating in the 1990s as a leader of the pharmaceutical sector, at a national level.

This is when the brand decided to renew its image and entrusted to Cruz Novillo the design of its visual identity. On this occasion, the designer used one of the universal codes to symbolise healing, the cross. With thick strokes, inscribing the cross within a circle, he produced a clear identity and unmistakable meaning, especially accompanied by the intense red colour palette.

Livery graphics for Indas.

International Year of Shelter for the Homeless

United Nations Organisation. International Union of Architects. 1986.

Campaña ¿usted fuma?

Campaign against smoking. 1978.

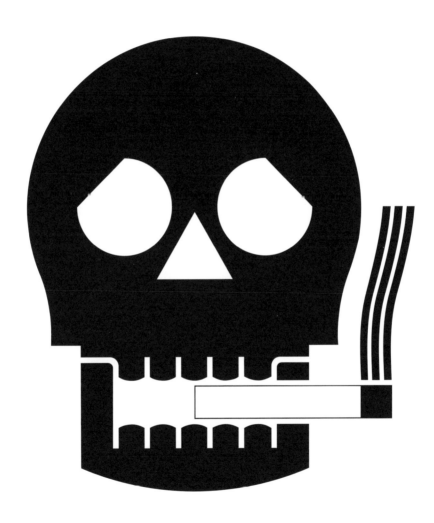

Berenguer Beneyto

Pharmaceutical laboratories. 1984.

Hotels

Cruz Novillo — Logos

Compañía Hotelera del Mediterráneo

Hotel company. 1971.

Hotels. 1971.

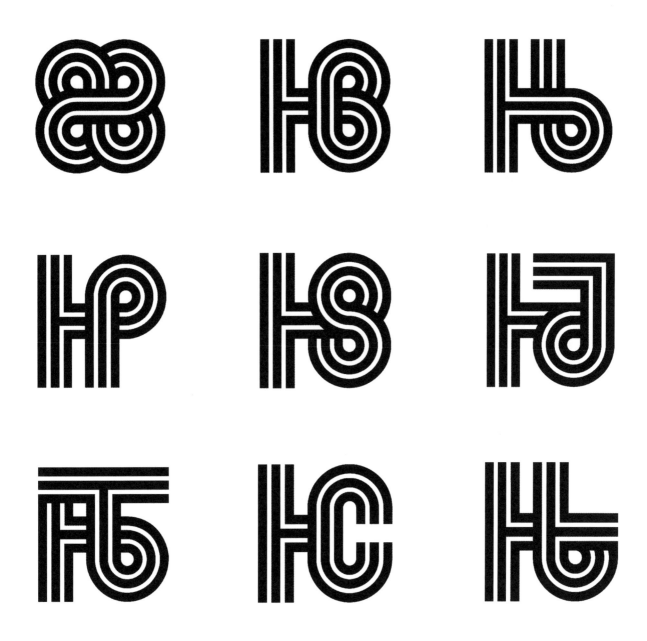

Iberhotel

Hotels. 1983.

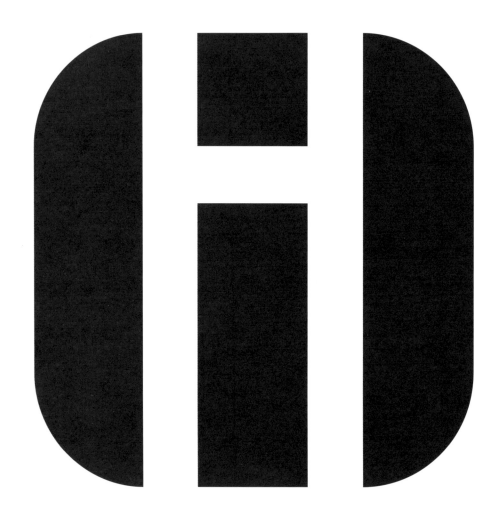

Hotels. 1988.

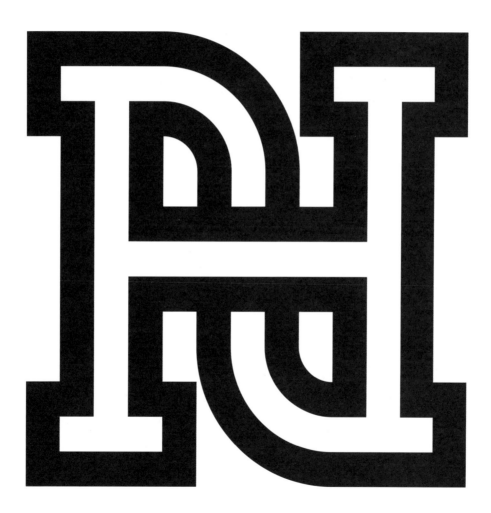

Apartamentos Galupe

Apartments. 1963.

Media

Cruz Novillo – Logos

TVE 1

In 1981, Cruz Novillo was commissioned to create the visual identity for the first Spanish television channel, with the intention of being implemented one year later to mark the celebration of the World Football Cup in Spain.

During that decade, TVE applied its visual identity in multiple ways: with flat colours, gradients, in three dimensions etc. The varied applications took advantage of the versatility of the symbol. From its composition consisting of a hexagon and a sphere, simple animations of great interest are created, still keeping in mind that the mark appears constantly in the lower right corner of the television screen.

Storyboard for digital animation. 1981.

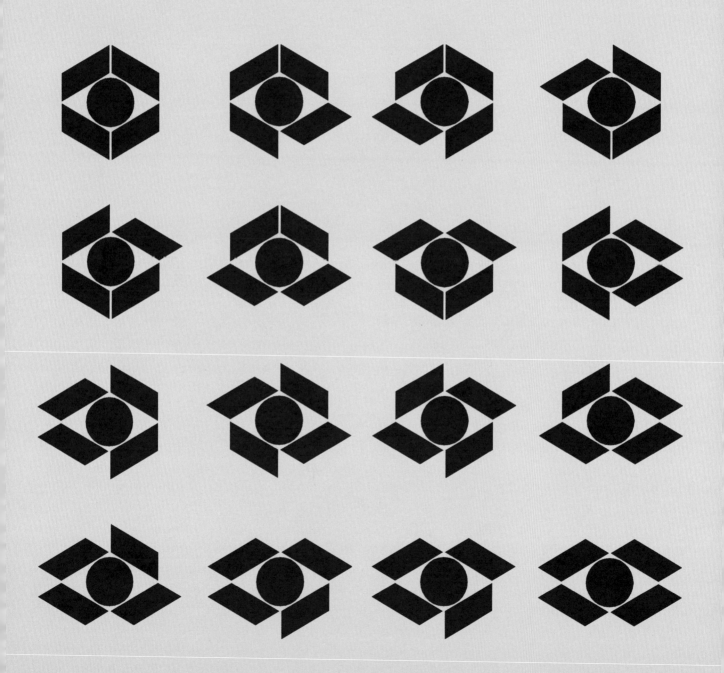

Timon

Media company. 1973.

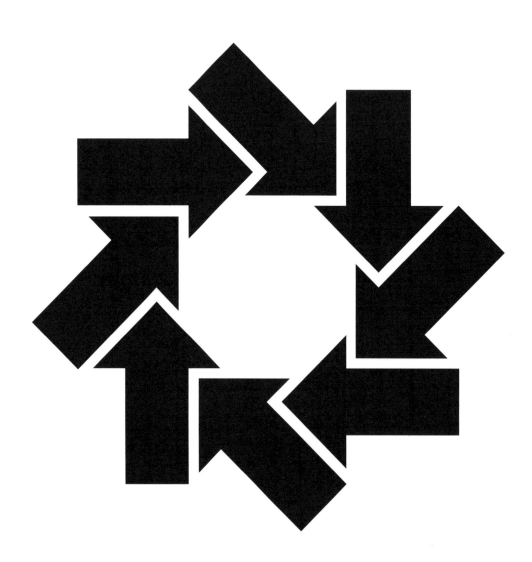

Editorial Mangold

Book publishers. 1969.

Canal de Editoriales

Publishing group. 1973.

Economy newspaper. 1993.

El Mundo

Newspaper. 1989.

EL MUNDO

The newspaper El Mundo was founded in 1989 by Juan Tomás de Salas and journalist Pedro J. Ramírez, who commissioned Cruz Novillo to create the masthead of the publication.

The designer created the symbol of a green sphere that represents the planet in a stylised, geometric form. This symbol is applied between the words 'El' and 'Mundo', which are composed with a serif typeface. The layout of the newspaper was made by Carmelo G. Caderot, who was art director for the newspaper 'Diario 16', for whom Cruz Novillo also designed the masthead. Years later, he also designed the newspapers 'La Gaceta de los Negocios' and 'El Economista', as well as the commission he has received since 1983 for the design of the 'El País Yearbook'.

On the occasion of the exhibition for the 25th anniversary of the newspaper in 2014, Cruz Novillo created a wooden sculpture and a series of multiple sculptures in stainless steel. He also proposed to print in 3D hundreds of thousands of sculptures that would be distributed with the newspaper on the day of the anniversary.

Sculpture for El Mundo.

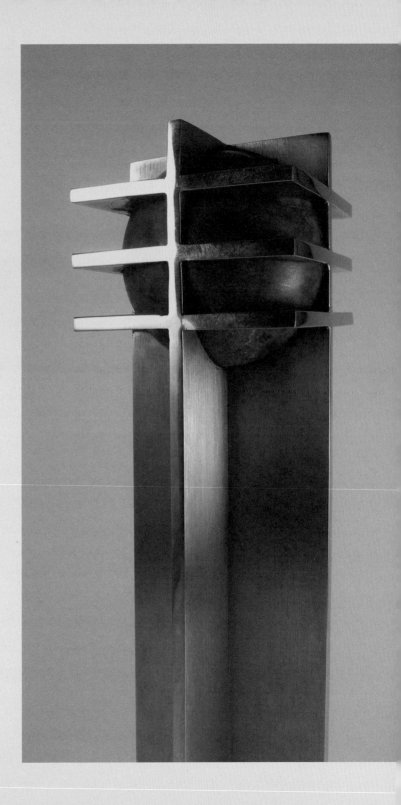

Impact

Marketing magazine. 1967.

Illustration for newspaper. 1979.

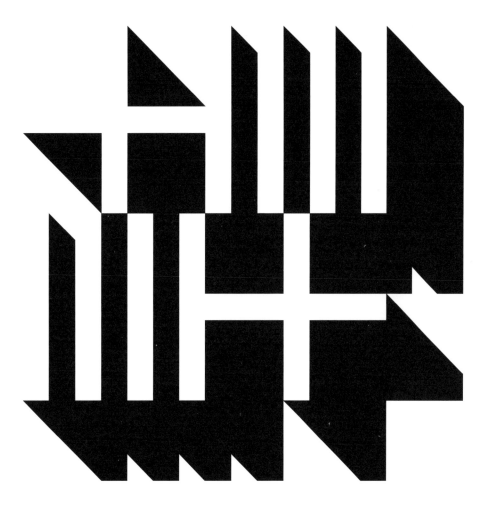

Creative Director: Enric Satué.

Masthead for El Economista.

EL ECONOMISTA

In 2005 the publisher Alfonso de Salas, with whom Cruz Novillo had already collaborated on the newspapers 'El Mundo' and 'Diario 16', commissioned him to design the visual identity for the newspaper 'El Economista'. Cruz Novillo created a masthead with elegant Bodoni typography and a colour palette of orange and black, referring to the salmon coloured pages of the economic press. He also made an abbreviated version of the 'eE' that functions as a symbol. In 2006, this project received the Society of News Design award for the world's best designed newspaper head.

Newspaper. 2005.

Creative Director: Soledad García de Viedma.

Temas de Marketing

Marketing magazine. 1979.

Ediciones Altea

Book publishers. 1972.

Jornadas de Marketing

Marketing days on advertising research. 1967.

School books of literature. 1976.

Cabitel

Telecommunications. 1990.

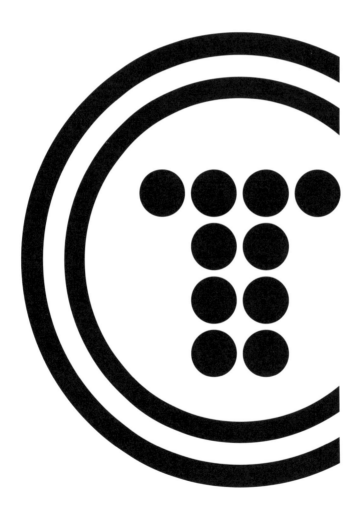

Audiovisual innovative initiatives. 1991.

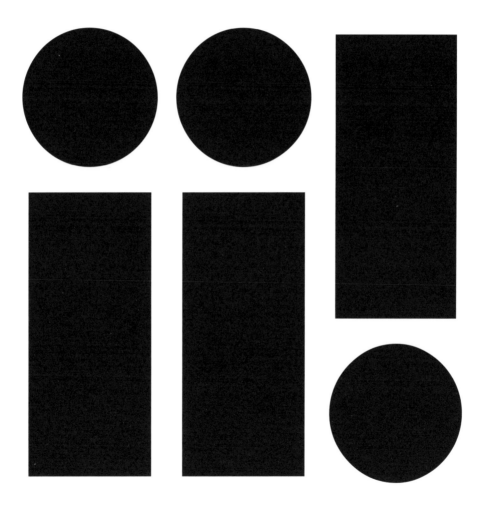

GRUPO PRISA

In 1990 the media group Prisa, the leader in its field in Spain, entrusted its visual identity to Cruz Novillo. During that time he carried out a number of other assignments for companies in the group, such as GMi Media Group, PrisaCom, Sogetel, Sogepaq and Idea etc.

The logo created by Cruz Novillo consists of a target, divided vertically into two halves, creating a striking positive and negative spacial tension. The main corporate colour is red and the secondary grey, which is used for the logotype. It is a family of marks in which Cruz Novillo's experience as a sculptor is evident, with a clear connection to his series of 'esculturas vacías', or 'empty sculptures', in which he explores the occupation and subtraction of space through the use of rectangular and semicircular shapes.

The designer's interest in the three-dimensional nature of the visual identities can be seen, for example, in the designs for the group's annual momentos, with the use of paper engineering and print techniques.

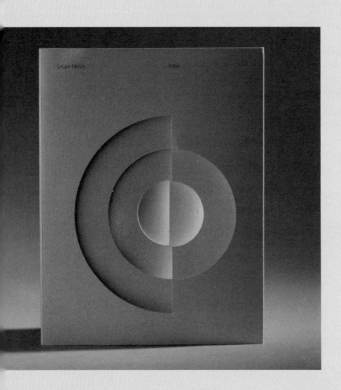

Grupo Prisa

Group of media companies. 1990.

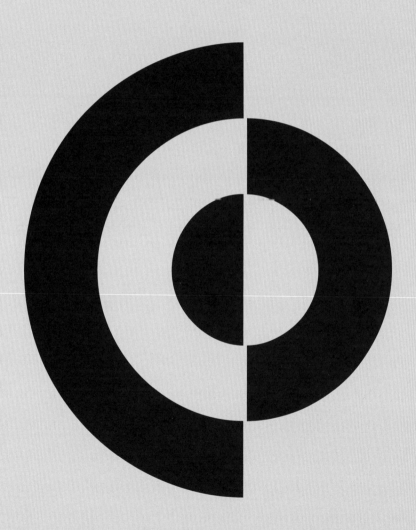

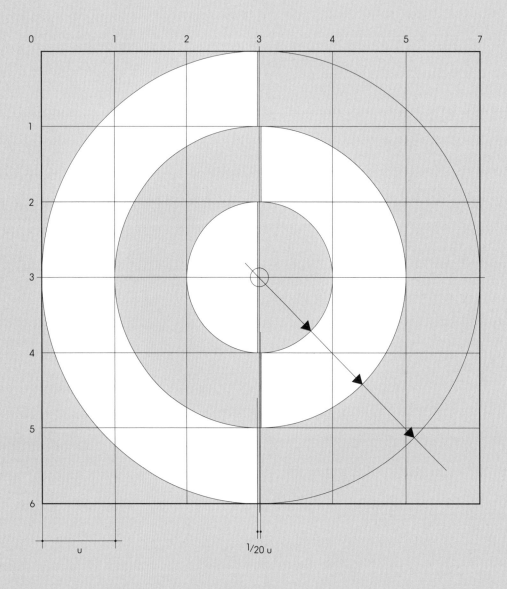

u

1/20 u

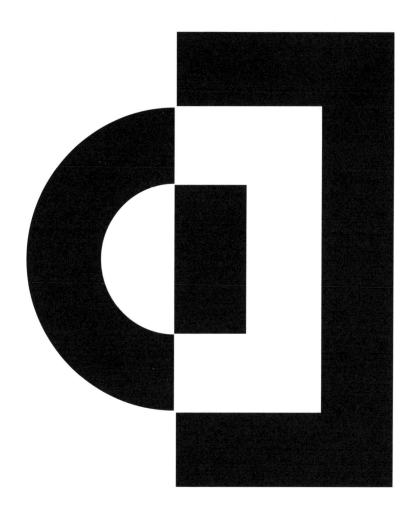

Grupo Prisa PrisaCom

Telecommunications. 1991.

Sogetel

Telecommunications company of Grupo Prisa. 1991.

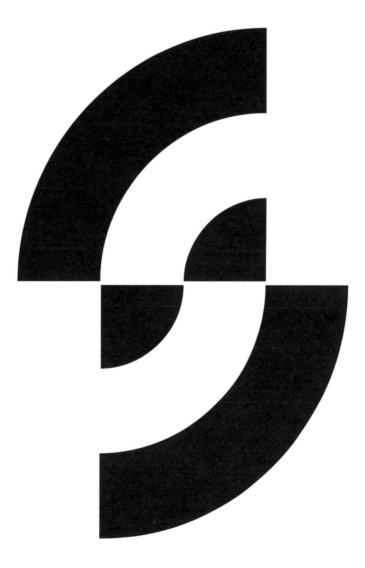

Sogepaq

Telecommunications company of Grupo Prisa. 1991.

Intelcom

Telecommunications. 1978.

Telefonica Star

Company of Telefonica Group. 1981.

Radio stations. 1993.

Cometa

Telecommunications. 1992.

Radio Guía

Radio stations guide. 1983.

Radio El País

Radio stations. 1984.

Antena 3

Radio stations. 1982.

Creative Director: José Antonio Loriga.

Stock

Audiovisual production company. 1984.

Stationery design
for Esicma.

Audiovisual production company. 1989.

El Ojo de la Cámara

Audiovisual production company. 1998.

Social
& Political

Cruz Novillo – Logos

PSOE. Partido Socialista Obrero Español

Spanish Socialist Party. 1977.

Vase sculpture for
PSOE, the Spanish
Socialist Party.

PSOE, PARTIDO SOCIALISTA OBRERO ESPAÑOL

Founded in 1879, 'Partido Socialista Obrero Español' – the Spanish Socialist Workers' Party – was forced to act clandestinely between 1939 and 1977, before it was finally legalised again. Parallel to many other institutions, with the advent of democracy, the PSOE decided to renew its visual identity.

Until then, the party used a pen, ink, book and anvil as a symbol. The emblem, born in the 1920s,

symbolised the union of physical and intellectual work. However, after the intervention of Cruz Novillo, the party ended up disconnecting from the old visual identity and opting instead for the fist and the rose, a symbol used internationally within socialism.

It first appeared in France in the early 1970s and soon began to be used by the socialist parties of Belgium, Chile and Spain and by the worldwide association of political parties 'Socialist International'. Cruz Novillo is quoted as saying that he wished

the organisation to step away from the inkwell and anvil because they represented a more 'esoteric symbolism'.

His work for the PSOE continues to represent the party 40 years later.

Recently, the designer has worked on a three dimensional version of the brand, which acts as a vase for a rose.

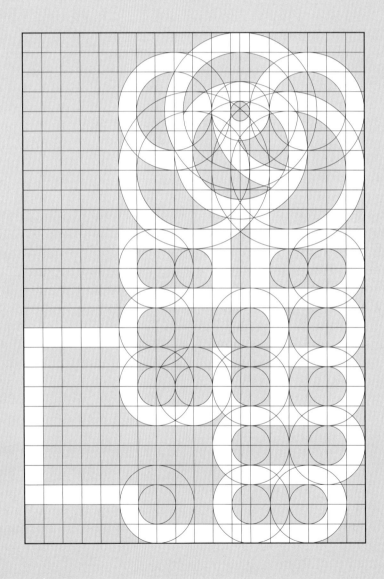

Pasoc

Political party. 1981.

Partido Andalucista

Political party. 1986.

Diputacion Provincial de Sevilla

DPS political administration. 1993.

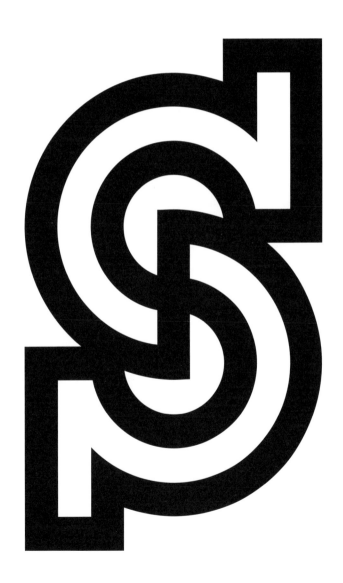

Euromed

Euro-mediterranean political conference. 1995.

Euromed bronze medals.

Euromed sculpture.

Junta Regional de Extremadura

Government of Extremadura region (Spain). 1978.

Technical commission of edification quality. 1976.

Fundación ONCE

Foundation for the disabled. 1988.

Fundación ONCE stationery.

FUNDACIÓN ONCE

The Fundación ONCE, set up for the cooperation with and social inclusion of people with disabilities, was born in 1988 and presents itself to society as an instrument of cooperation and solidarity with the Spanish blind and other groups of people with disabilities to improve their living conditions.

Cruz Novillo was commissioned to create its visual identity, which became one of the most widely used logos in Spain and is still in use. It consists of two interlacing double circles in red, symbolising a united solidarity between equals. It can also be seen as two letter 'O's or even two eyes.

The brand is especially attractive when it is implemented in the form of a three-dimensional sign, as it appears in the headquarters of the Foundation.

OTAN

Sculpture project for Nato summit in Madrid. 1996.

ADE Asociación de Diplomáticos Españoles

The Association of Spanish Diplomats. 1993.

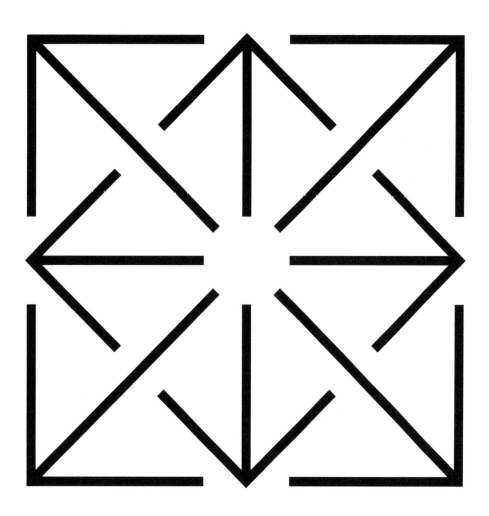

Multiple bronze sculpture
for Fundación Teneo.

Foundation for the defense of the environment. 1995.

Correos

Spanish postal service. 1977.

CORREOS

In 1976, the 'Dirección General de Correos y Telégrafos' commissioned Clarín Advertising to renew its visual identity and it would be Cruz Novillo, who left the agency ten years previously, who would be responsible for carrying out this prestigious project. The branding is now considered, by some experts, to be the first great transformation of the image of a public body since the arrival of democracy in Spain.

For the new identity, the designer created a symbol that consists of a crowned cornet, realised with the thick, geometric traits characteristic of Pepe at this time. It was the first royal crown designed specifically for the visual identity of a Spanish public company.

The symbol was accompanied by the text 'Correos y Telégrafos', which translates as 'Post and Telegraphs' and is composed with a very stylised, italic typography, provoking a strong contrast with the voluminous strokes of the symbol. As for the colour palette, a combination of yellow and red was chosen, alluding to the Spanish flag. Years later, Cruz Novillo was commissioned to redesign this brand, this time opting for white and yellow, a combination of low contrast colours that the designer considered appropriate, due to the enormous implementation of the brand throughout the country.

The choice of a cornet and the colour yellow for the post office identity was not arbitrary. The origin of these elements dates back to the 16th century, when the Tasso family created one of the first European postal services. This symbology continues today in other countries such as Germany and Italy.

The visual identity of Correos won the Laus Prize in 1978.

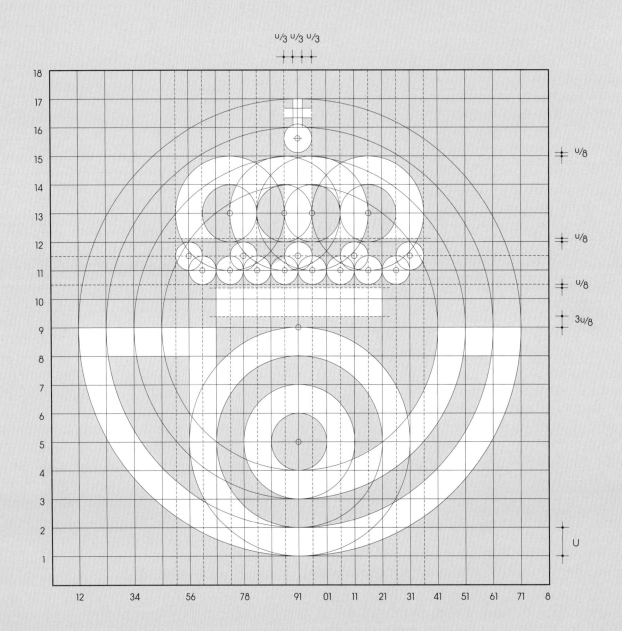

Correos livery graphics.

Correos signage.

Mail bag design.

Mail box logo implementation.

SUN Socorro Urgente a los Necesitados

Emergency services. 1995.

Ministerio de Educación y Ciencia

Ministry of Education & Science. 1985.

Cuerpo Nacional de Policía

Spanish National Police. 1986.

CUERPO NACIONAL DE POLICÍA

The commission for the renewal of the identity of the Spanish National Police is one of the most important projects that Cruz Novillo has worked on. The institution sought to renew not only the visual identity, but also the design of uniforms and their accessories, the fleet of vehicles, signage of police stations, systems of badges and more. Luckily, Cruz Novillo had a network of talent, with experts in different areas who advised him on such a large task.

As for the visual identity, one of the most radical changes occurred in the colour pallette. Cruz Novillo substituted the old brown colour of the uniforms for navy blue, in one of the decisions that the designer considers one of high importance to the overall task.

The official police shield is complex in terms of the number of elements that configure it, but simple in its reading thanks to the contrast of postive and negative spacial areas that produce its strokes. It is still used today, decades after it was designed, without any change.

Ciudad de Granada

Manuel de Falla auditorium. 1982.

Sotogrande

Port in Cádiz. 1964.

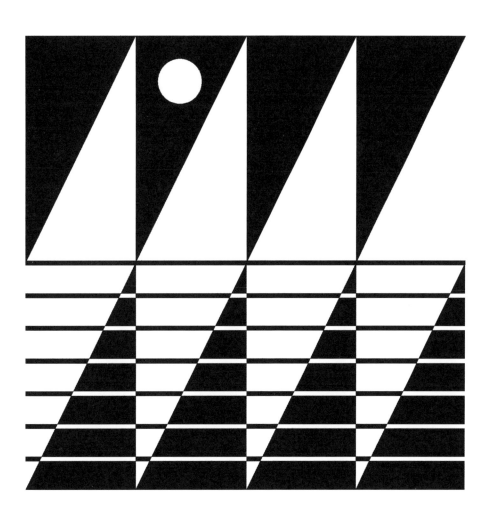

España 2002

Promotion campaign. 2001.

Comunidad de Madrid

Community of Madrid. 1985.

Sculpture.

Comunidad de Madrid
T-shirts.

Sport trophies.

Comunidad de Madrid

Community of Madrid. Coat of arms. 1984.

COMUNIDAD DE MADRID

For the former president of Madrid, Joaquín Leguina, Cruz Novillo created a visual identity for the region: a shield and a flag that were presented in 1984.

Cruz Novillo worked with the poet, art critic and history expert Santiago Amón, in order to create the identity, with Amón in charge of the historical investigation that was required by such a project.

The new shield sought to convey the essence of the newly formed Community of Madrid and for that reason all the elements have a meaning:

Colour: The bottom of the shield is red, referring to the flag of Castilla, symbolising the Castilian ancestry of the community.

Castles: Representative of the union of the two Castillas, the reference was taken from an old coat of arms from 1922. The colour yellow is used and sometimes gold.

Stars: Both castles are overlaid by seven five-pointed stars aligned in two rows, which are an allusion to the constellation of the Little Bear, very visible in the sky of Madrid. The five points make reference to the five provinces within the community: Avila, Segovia, Guadalajara, Cuenca and Toledo.

Corona: At the top there is a yellow crown that identifies the capital as 'Real Sitio' and indicates that it is the place of residence of the king.

The design of the flag is simpler, with the same red colour from the shield and the seven stars of the Little Bear divided into horizontal blocks, four stars above and three below.

Corporate guidelines for Comunidad de Madrid.

INC Instituto Nacional de Consumo

National consumption institute. 1986.

Municipal consumer information offices. 1986.

Ayuntamiento de Madrid

City of Madrid integrated management systems. 2017.

Creative Director: Pepe Cruz.

Sport

Cruz Novillo — Logos

Coca-Cola Cups

Children's sports competitions. 1979

Coca-Cola Cup
T-shirt & keychain.

Coca-Cola Cups

Children's sports competitions. 1979

Real Madrid

Foundation of Real Madrid football club. 1991.

Campaign materials
for Espíritu Olímpico,
the International
Olympic Committee.

Espíritu Olímpico. International Olympic Committee

Campaign against violence in sports. 1994.

Golf Escorpión

Golf club. 1969.

Golf La Moraleja

Golf club. 1974.

Patinopolis

Skating track. 1983.

opolis

El Abuelo

Guns & sports shop. 1967.

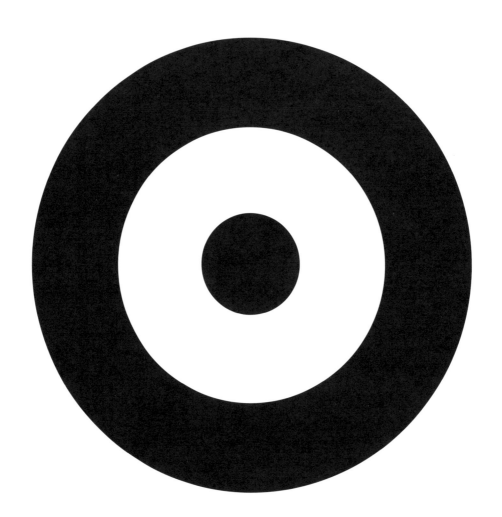

Technology

Cruz Novillo – Logos

Micronica

Computers. 1982.

Computers. 1977.

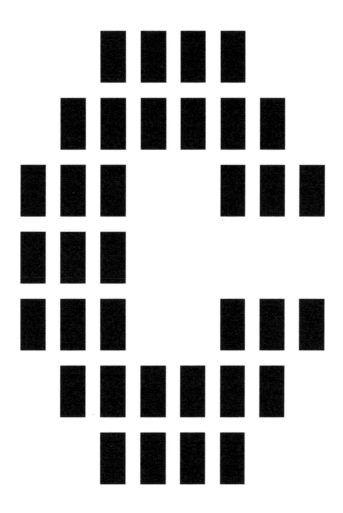

Inves

Computers by El Corte Inglés. 1994.

Cindus Audiosistemas

Audio systems company. 1972.

Cindus Videosistemas

Video systems company. 1972.

Micro

Computers. 1992.

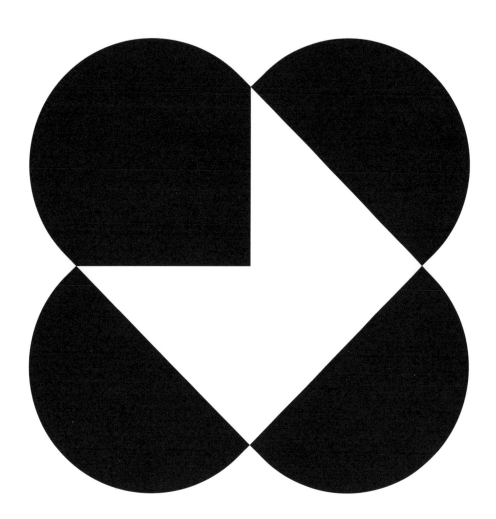

Cdti Prize

Industrial & technological development. 1982.

Cdti

Industrial technological development centre. 1980.

Transport & Travel

Cruz Novillo — Logos

Prodespaña

Export company. 1981.

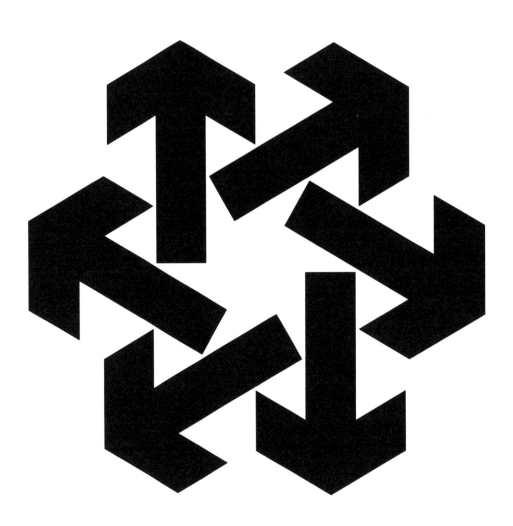

Norte

Travel agency. 1980.

Transsa

Transports group. 1969.

Enatcar

Bus transport company. 1996.

Train & station graphics for Renfe.

RENFE

In the 80s, Renfe required a new change of image and contacted Cruz Novillo to carry out the commission. The designer faced a large project, which included the visual identity and signage for both Renfe and other companies within the group.

For the creation of the new brand, Cruz Novillo started with the existing design, created by Juan Toribio in 1971. One of the contributions that Cruz Novillo made was to redraw and simplify the previous symbol, by eliminating the circular border that surrounded it and shortening the arrows, which now no longer reached the edge of the circumference. The colour palette was also modified, the yellow

became the secondary colour, with the visual identity applied in dark blue. In terms of typography, Cruz Novillo retained the existing capital letters but eliminated the reference to train tracks by introducing a simpler and more forceful typography.

A major project challenge was the creation and implementation of a new train station signaling system for such a large and complex company at a time when computer use was not yet widespread. Cruz Novillo had to draw hundreds of pictograms for the new system, each inscribed in a circular holding device, to be used in thousands of stations and installations of Renfe.

The project lasted for five years and in addition to the identity

and signage, application of the graphic pattern in print, trains and advertising were defined.

During the 1990s, Cruz Novillo continued to work for the brand, performing identity and signage work for Paquexpres, Renfe and Renfe Regional Stations, even designing the interiors and exteriors of some trains. Each of these works was described in detail in at least one corporate identity manual.

In the year 2000 Renfe decided to renew its visual identity and again came to Cruz Novillo to redesign his own work. The range of colours were simplified, the symbol adopted a lighter blue and the previous typography was replaced by a serif face in italics, that showed the mark, for the first time in a long while, in lowercase.

Renfe

National Spanish railways. 1987.

Paquexpres Renfe

Spanish parcel transportation railways. 1990.

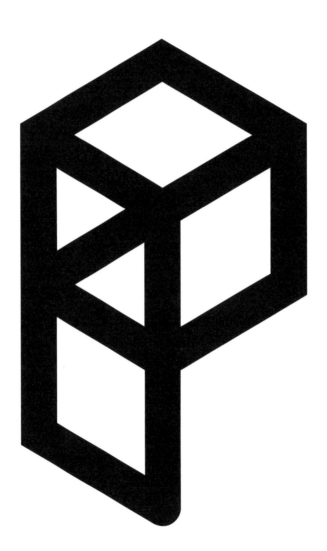

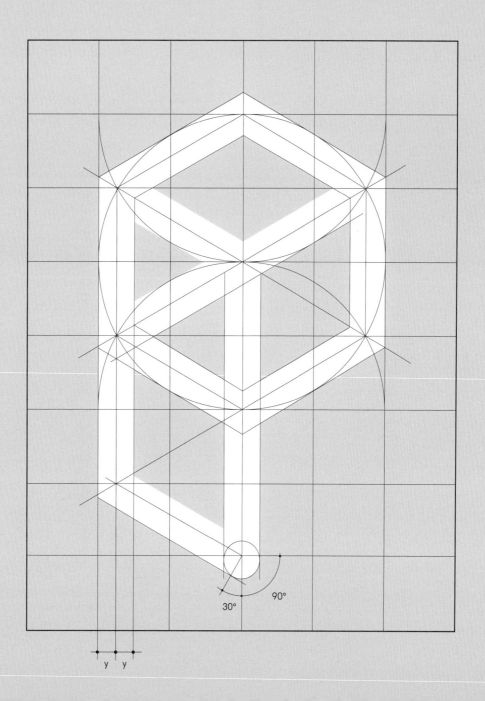

30° 90°

y y

Train graphics for
Paquexpres Renfe.

Train graphics for
Renfe Regionales.

Renfe Regionales

National Spanish railways (short range). 1991.

Aero Andalucia

Aviation company. 1984.

Aeresa

Aviation component factory. 1984.

Sculpture for Ausa
Autopistas Argentinas.

Ausa Autopistas Argentinas

Argentine highways. 1974.

Intersol Viajes

Travel agency. 1977.

Seidacar

Motorhomes. 1974.

Costa del Sol

Costa del Sol promotion. 1974.

Tour operator. 1993.

Dirección General de Tráfico

General direction of traffic. 1962.

Pepe Cruz

Designer & Architect.

Personal photographs
from Pepe Cruz Novillo Jnr.

To start at the beginning, did you grow up in a household surrounded by art?_____ Yes, my mother Amelia Jiménez is also an artist, who specialised in patchwork and collage. I grew up in an environment that was very different from the one of my friends at school. I have the feeling that artists are special people, with quite different priorities in life in comparison with the rest of human beings. I saw my father drawing all the time, both at his board at home and in his studio. And he always had a notebook to draw portraits and cityscapes; I still keep some of them. I think I never asked him about his profession, although I noticed that the parents of my friends had different jobs, and dressed in a more formal way. And none of them rode a Harley Davidson!

Later on, how were you encouraged to pursue a creative career yourself?_____ I never felt pressured by my parents to continue in their professional footsteps, although I never wanted to devote myself to anything else. When I discovered my father was the creator of many brands that I saw walking down the street, I thought that this was the job I wanted to exercise. At the age of 18, I asked him directly what should I study to be like him and he said, 'architecture'. It's the best advice he has ever given me. I became an architect and since then combine both professions, which aren't so different, by the way.

Why do you think his work is so successful?_____ Let me answer with all sincerity: because he is a genius. I think that many of his works are simply unbeatable. That's the reason why they endure so many decades with full force, because they are the result of bright concepts masterfully drawn.

What do you think about the renewed interest in your father's work today?_____ I'm very happy, but not surprised. What is a big surprise, is that the first great book about Cruz Novillo, an 80 year old Spanish designer, has been edited outside of Spain. I have high hopes that this book is going to be very important for the global broadcasting of the work of Cruz Novillo. Hopefully, future publications will focus on his impressive work as an Illustrator, poster designer and artist.

Cruz Novillo

Sculptor & Designer.

BIOGRAPHY

Born in Cuenca in 1936. In 1957 abandons his studies in the Faculty of Law and starts working as a cartoonist at Clarín Advertising, living since then in Madrid. In 1959 begins to collaborate as an industrial designer in SEDI (society of industrial design studies) and four years later he is selected to form part of the team of artists for the Pavilion of Spain at the world fair of New York.

In 1965, performing the role of Creative Director, he abandons Clarín and opens his own design studio, creating since then, amongst many others, the corporate images of institutions and companies such as Correos, Banco Pastor, Portland Valderrivas, Urbis, Entrecanales, Tesoro Público, the coat of arms and the flag of Comunidad de Madrid, PSOE, COPE, Grupo PRISA, Diario 16, El Mundo, El Economista, La Gaceta de los Negocios, Antena 3 Radio, Endesa, Inves, Construcciones y Contratas, Huarte, Ministerio de Educación y Ciencia, Icex, Red Eléctrica, Quinto Centenario del Descubrimiento de América, Billetes del Banco de España, Renfe, La Noche en Blanco, Bicentenario de la Guerra de la Independencia, Visionlab, Cuenca 2016, Fundación ONCE and Repsol.

His studio Cruz más Cruz (that he co-directs with his son Pepe Cruz, architect) has won the restricted contest for the design of the corporate identity of the Government of Spain (still unpublished).

He has designed the posters for films such as El Sur, El Espíritu de la Colmena, Pascual Duarte [1], El Desengaño, Cría Cuervos, Historias del Kronen, Las Cartas de Alou, Una Estación de Paso, Mamá cumple 100 años, La Escopeta Nacional [2], Hay que matar a B., Familia, Barrio, Los Lunes al Sol, El hombre que diseñó España and many others.

He has been the president of the Spanish Association of Professional Designers (AEPD), of which he is Honorary Member, as well as Dimad

1.
Poster for the film 'Pascual Duarte' (1976). Director: Ricardo Franco.

—

2.
Poster for the film 'La escopeta nacional' (1978). Director: Luis G. Berlanga.

3.

4.

5.

3.
'Diafragma Tres' (1995). Exhibition
& piano concert in Sala Luzán
(Zaragoza). Pianist: David
López Cruz.
—
4.
'Diafragma Heptafónico 823.543,
opus 9' (1998). Museum of Real
Academia de BB.AA. de San
Fernando (Madrid).
—
5.
'Diafragma Decafónico de Dígitos'
(2006). Façade of the Statistics
National Institute (Madrid).

3.

361.

association in Madrid. He is Visiting Professor at Universidad Francisco de Vitoria, Universidad Internacional Menéndez Pelayo and the school of architecture of Universidad Politécnica de Madrid.

In 1972 he made an exhibition in Skira Gallery (Madrid), exhibiting since then regularly his paintings, sculptures, engravings.

In 1977 he participated with a 'one man show' at the International Art Biennial of São Paulo (Brasil).

He has participated in the art fairs FIAC (Paris), Bassel Art, Art Cologne and in ARCO (Madrid) in an almost uninterrupted way since 1985.

José María Cruz Novillo is an artist with a professional career spanning over fifty years. Since the early 90s it has been centered on the development of the concept 'Diafragma' [3,4] (diaphragm), that encompasses several works whose common feature is the combination of a variable number of monochromatic, sound, photographic or three-dimensional elements.

In 2008 he finished his 'Diafragma Decafónico de Dígitos' [5] in the facade of the Instituto Nacional de Estadística flagship building in Madrid, where once again the sound is part of the artwork, translating statistical indicators to a language of colours and musical notes in a synesthetic way.

The 22nd of May of 2009 was the premiere of his concert 'Diafragma heptafónico 49, opus 13' (7 minutes in duration) during his entry speech at San Fernando Royal Academy of Fine Arts. His 'Diafragma dodecafónico 8.916.100.448.256, opus 14', (3.390.410 years in duration, starting on the 17th February 2010) contains all the combinations with the repetition of 12 colours, 12 musical notes and 12 fragments of time. It can be followed live, until its completion, at www.cruznovilloopus14.com. The closing day, a cocktail will be served.

Awards & Distinctions

Laus Prize for the design of Correos visual identity 1978.

National Design Prize 1997.

AEPD Prize 1993, 1995, 1996 and 2001.

CCM National Painting Prize 2002.

FAD Medal 2006.

Society of News Design Prize to the best designed newspaper header (El Economista) 2006.

Castilla-La Mancha Design Prize 2008.

Gold Medal of Merit in the Fine Arts 2012.

Gráffica Design Prize 2017.

Correos Honorary Postman 2019.

Academic of San Fernando Royal Academy of Fine Arts.

Individual Art Exhibitions

1972 Galería Skira. Madrid.

1977 "Un pintor, un escultor". Canogar, Cruz Novillo. Galería AELE. Madrid.
—
XIV Bienal de Sao Paulo.

1980 "Pinturas, esculturas, dibujos y collages". Galería AELE. Madrid.

1984 Escuela de Arquitectura de la Universidad de Navarra.

1985 One man show. Pinturas y Esculturas. ARCO '85. Galería AELE. Madrid.

1986 BASEL ART '86. Galería AELE. Basilea.

1987 FIAC '87. Galería AELE. París.
—
"Pinturas y Esculturas". Galería AELE. Madrid.

1988 Galería Artline. La Haya.
—
Galería Tórculo. Madrid.

1989 ARCO '89. Galería AELE. Madrid.
—
Dípticos y Esculturas "Ciclo La Haya". Galería AELE. Madrid.
—
ART COLOGNE '89. Galería AELE. Colonia.

1991 "Pinturas y Esculturas". Galería AELE. Madrid.
—
BASEL ART '91. Galería AELE. Basilea.

1992 Museo Barjola. Gijón.

1993 Obra gráfica. Galería Tórculo. Madrid.
—
280 Proyectos y 70 Esculturas Plegables del ciclo "Diafragma Dos". Galería AELE. Madrid.

1994 One man show. ARCO '94. Galería AELE. Madrid.

1995 Galería Anselmo Alvarez. Madrid.

1997 "Un, dos, tres, cuatro dimensiones". Esculturas. Galería AELE-Evelyn Botella. Madrid.

1999 "Obra reciente". Galería AELE-Evelyn Botella. Madrid.
—
"Obras 1980–1999". Casa del Cordón. Burgos.

2000 "Obras 1980–1999". Sala Amós Salvador. Logroño.

2001 "Diafragma Rainbow". Galería AELE-Evelyn Botella. Madrid.
—
"Diafragma Rainbow". Colegio de Arquitectos de Málaga.

2002 "Diafragma Rainbow".

Fundación Antonio Pérez. Cuenca.

2003 "Diafragma Tres". Sala Luzán. Zaragoza.

2004 "Stripes". Galería AELE-Evelyn Botella. Madrid.

2005 "Stripes". Galería Tolmo. Toledo.

2006 "Canciones". Galería AELE-Evelyn Botella. Madrid.

2008 "Still Life for Cezanne". Feria Casa Pasarela. Stand Berceli. Madrid.
—
Concierto "Diafragma heptafónico 3.612, opus 12", para corno inglés. Siete horas de duración. Patio central del Centro Conde Duque. La Noche en Blanco. Madrid.
—
"Chair". Galería Evelyn Botella. Madrid.
—
"Diafragma hexafónico Chair". B.d. Madrid.
—
"Diafragma Skull". Galería Serie. Madrid.

2009 "Diafragma heptafónico 49, opus 13", para corno inglés. Siete minutos de duración. Estrenado en el discurso de ingreso de Cruz Novillo en la Real Academia de Bellas Artes de San Fernando.

2011 "Diafragma heptafónico 823.543, opus 9". Ciclo "El Artista ante su Obra". Museo de la Real Academia de Bellas Artes de San Fernando. Madrid.

2012 "T-Selfportraits by Cruz Novillo". Galería Evelyn Botella. Madrid.

2015 "T-Selfportraits by Cruz Novillo". Real Academia de BB.AA. de San Fernando. Madrid.
—
"Tribute to Morandi d'après Zurbarán". Museo Thyssen. Madrid.

"Diafragma dodecafónico
8.916.100.448.256, opus 14".
Club Matador. Madrid.
—
"Diafragma dodecafónico
8.916.100.448.256, opus 14" y
"Diafragma hexafónico Chair, opus 11".
Museo Patio Herreriano. Valladolid.
—
"La cuadratura del círculo". Espacio
DiLab. Urueña, Valladolid.

2016 "Diafragma heptafónico para Cuenca
2016, opus 9". Teatro-Auditorio de
Cuenca. Cuenca.

2017 "Videomapping for the façade
of Universidad de Salamanca".
Festival de Luz y Vanguardias.
Salamanca.

2018 "Cruz Novillo. Obras
cronocromofónicas". Museo Francisco
Sobrino. Guadalajara.
—
"Cruz Novillo. La cuadratura del
círculo". Galería Vilaseco. A Coruña.
—
"Cruz Novillo. Esculturas de tiempo,
espacio, luz, sonido, bronce,
aluminio, madera y papel". Galería
Espacio Primavera 9. Madrid.

2019 "La cuadratura del círculo". Cosentino
City. Madrid.
—
"Cronocromofonía". Galería Fernando
Pradilla. Espacio Proyectos. Madrid.
—
"Primeros 60 años de arte y diseño".
Casa Zavala. Cuenca.

2019 "La cuadratura del círculo". Museo de
San Clemente. Cuenca.
—
"Diafragma dodecafónico, opus 14.
Canciones". Fundación Antonio Pérez.
Cuenca.
—
"Diafragma Tres Mata-Hari".

Marta Moriarty art window. Madrid.

2020 "Cruz Novillo: cronocromofonía (obras
de tiempo, color y sonido)". ARCO'20.
Stand de El Mundo. Madrid.
—
"Cruz Novillo. Las dos dimensiones
y media. Obras de la Bienal de
Sao Paulo, 1977". Galería Fernando
Pradilla. Madrid.

2021 "Cruz Novillo". Palacio Quintanar.
Segovia.

Collective Art Exhibitions

1972 "Originales y múltiples". Caja de
Ahorros de Navarra. Santillana del
Mar. Santander.

1973 Colegio de Arquitectos de Canarias.
Santa Cruz de Tenerife.

1974 Galería Múltiple 4.17. Madrid.
—
1ª Exposición de Escultura al Aire
Libre. Madrid.

1977 "Forma y medida en el Arte Español.
Biblioteca Nacional. Madrid.

1978 "Pintura Española Contemporánea".
Fundación Gulbenkian. Lisboa.
—
"Pintura Española Contemporánea".
La Habana.
—
"Escultura en el jardín". Madrid.
—
"Artistas españoles en la Bienal de
Sao Paulo". Galería Grifé y Escoda.
Madrid.

1980 "El Collage". Galería AELE. Madrid.
—
"Abstracción Geométrica". Itinerante
por España.

1983 "Experimentación en el Arte".
Sala Conde Duque. Madrid.

"Arte e información". SIMO. Casa de
Campo. Madrid.

1984 "La cultura de Castilla-La Mancha y sus
raíces". Palacio de Velázquez. Madrid.

"Arte y Nuevas Tecnologías".
Universidad Internacional Menéndez
Pelayo. Santander.

"El Pacto Invisible". Galería AELE.
Madrid.

1985 "El Pacto Invisible". Sala Luzán.
Zaragoza.
—
"El Pacto Invisible". Galería Ciento.
Barcelona.
—
"Propuestas Objetivas". Galería
Fernando Vijande. Madrid.
—
"Propuestas Objetivas". Caja de León.
León.

1986 "Nuevas Formas y Construcción".
Galería AELE. Madrid.
—
"Propuestas Objetivas". Casa de
Cultura. Zamora.
—
FIAC '86. Galería Denise René. París.
—
I Bienal Iberoamericana de Arte
Seriado. Sevilla.

1987 "El Pacto Invisible". ARCO '87. Galería
AELE. Madrid.

Centro Cultural Conde Duque.
Madrid.
—
"Constructivistas Españoles". Caja
de Ahorros de Córdoba. Madrid.
—
"Homenaje al Cubismo". Facultad
de Bellas Artes. Madrid.

1988 FIAC '88. Galería AELE.

1989 "Arte Geométrico en España 1957–1989". Centro Cultural de la Villa. Madrid.

1990 "15". Galería AELE. Madrid.

1991 ARCO '91. Galería AELE. Madrid.

1992 ARCO '92. Galería Tórculo. Madrid.

"Forma y Conceptos. Esculturas". Estudio Theo. Sala Celini. Madrid.

1993 "Cuadros de una exposición". Galería AELE. Madrid.

1994 "Arriba y abajo". Galería AELE. Madrid.

Julián Gil, José María Iglesias y Cruz Novillo. Caja Provincial de Ahorros de Córdoba.

1996 "El nacimiento de una ilusión". 100 años de cine/20 años Galería AELE. Galería AELE-Evelyn Botella. Madrid.
—
ARCO '96. Galería AELE-Evelyn Botella. Madrid.

1997 "a Evelyn". Galería AELE-Evelyn Botella. Madrid.

1999 ARCO '99. Galería AELE-Evelyn Botella. Madrid.
—
"La medida armónica". Galería Edurne. Madrid.

2000 ARCO '00. Galería AELE-Evelyn Botella. Madrid.
—
"Puntos de vista". Galería Sandunga. Granada.
—
"El Pacto Visible". Galería AELE-Evelyn Botella. Madrid.

2001 ARCO '01. Galería AELE-Evelyn Botella. Madrid.

"Memoria y Modernidad". Arte y Artistas del Siglo XX en Castilla-La Mancha. Exposición itinerante.
—
"Expresiones exactas". Diputación de Zamora. Zamora.

2002 ARCO '02. Galería AELE-Evelyn Botella. Madrid.

"Reds". Galería AELE-Evelyn Botella. Madrid.

"Mirando los 70". Galería AELE-Evelyn Botella. Madrid.

2003 "Sin límites". Diputación de Zaragoza. Palacio de Sástago. Zaragoza.

ARCO '03. Galería AELE-Evelyn Botella. Madrid.
—
"Sin límites". Centro Cultural Cajastur. Palacio de Revillagigedo. Gijón.

"Encuentros". Palacio de Santa Cruz. Junta de Castilla-La Mancha. Toledo.
—
"Expresiones exactas". Centro Puerta de Toledo. Madrid.
—
V Edición Premios Ángel de Pintura. Alcázar de los Reyes Cristianos. Córdoba.

2004 ARCO '04. Galería AELE-Evelyn Botella. Madrid.

2005 ARCO '05. Galería AELE-Evelyn Botella. Madrid.
—
"Viceversa". Galería AELE-Evelyn Botella. Madrid.
—
"Trente ans après". Galería AELE-Evelyn Botella. Madrid.

2006 ARCO '06. Galería AELE-Evelyn Botella. Madrid.

"Escultura: Sempere, Oteiza, Cruz Novillo...". Galería Quorum. Madrid.

2007 ARCO '07. Galería AELE-Evelyn Botella. Madrid.

2008 "Diafragma hexafónico Chair". Feria Casa Pasarela. Madrid.

2010 ARCO '10. Galería Evelyn Botella. Madrid.

"Escultura: Feliciano, Caruncho, Cruz Novillo...". Galería Quorum. Madrid.

"Escultores Contemporáneos: Chirino, Rueda, Torner, Serrano, Mompó, Cruz Novillo...". El bosque de Acero.

Espacio Moneo. Cuenca.

2011 "36 años de Cultura en libertad". Fundación Caja Castilla La Mancha. Cuenca.

2013 "Modulares: Rueda, Equipo 57, Cruz Novillo, Max Bill, Pérez Villalta, F.Ll.Wright, Ron Arad, Schlosser". Galería Rafael Ortiz. Sevilla.
—
"El Papel de la Movida". Museo ABC. Madrid.

2014 "Forever Young. Diafragma dodecafónico 8.916.100.448.256, opus 14". Matadero. Madrid.
—
"La mano en el pecho de El Greco". Tolmo Museum. Toledo.

"El Mundo 25 años". Centro Conde Duque. Madrid.

"El trabajo de lo visible". Galería Odalys. Madrid.

"Territorios des-habitados". Galería El Pacto Invisible. Málaga.

2015 "60 Anys de Geometria".

Museu Universitat D'Alacant. Alicante.

"Geometrías". Galería El Pacto Invisible. Málaga.

"Entre la Ciència i la Ficció". Galería Octubre. Universitat Jaume I. Castellón.

2016 "Luz y Vanguardias". Video mapping sobre la fachada del Ayuntamiento de Salamanca.

"Escuchar con los ojos. Arte sonoro en España 1961–2016". Fundación Juan March. Madrid.

2017 "Arte en Palacio. 30 años de exposiciones en la Casa del Cordón". Casa del Cordón. Burgos.

"Homo Ludens". APgallery. Riaza. Segovia.

"Otras geometrías". Espacio DiLab. Urueña. Valladolid.

2018 "Kimono Joya, T de kimono". Casa de subastas Setdart. Valencia.

2019 "Un lugar inventado/An invented place". Ámbito Cultural El Corte Inglés. Madrid.

"Kimono Joya". Embajada de España en Tokyo. Japón.

"El juego del arte. Pedagogías, arte y diseño". Fundación Juan March. Madrid.

"La arteinformada curated by Miryam Anllo Vento". Espacio DiLab. Urueña. Valladolid.

"Estructura manipulable". Galería Fernando Pradilla. Feria Estampa. Madrid.

2020 "Obras de la Bienal de Sao Paulo'77".

ARCO'20. Stand de la Galería Fernando Pradilla. Madrid.

"Derivas de la imaginación. Otras visiones de la geometría". Galería Odalys. Madrid.

2021 "Escultura". Galería Fernando Pradilla. Feria Estampa. Madrid.

Museums & Art Collections

Museo Nacional Centro de Arte Reina Sofía.

Museo de Arte Contemporáneo de Sevilla.

Museo de Arte Contemporáneo de Villafamés.

Museo de Arte Contemporáneo de Tánger.

Museo Patio Herreriano de Valladolid.

Museo Real Academia de Bellas Artes de San Fernando.

Fundación Juan March.

Collection Centro Conde Duque.

Collection Caja de Burgos.

Collection Caja Castilla-La Mancha.

Collection Sala Luzán.

Collection Alfonso Cortina.

Collection José Lladó.

Collection Pilar Citoler.

Collection Rafael Canogar.

Collection Accenture.

Collection La Caixa.

Sculptures in Public & Private Spaces

Stainless steel sculpture. 3,50×3,50×3,00m. Edificio Bancaya. Madrid.

Manipulate panel. 13,50×4,00m. Edificio Campsa. Madrid.

Stainless steel relief with enamel. 8,00×3,50m. Banco de España. Madrid.

Stainless steel relief. 20,00×11,00m. Fachada del Hotel Los Lebreros. Sevilla.

Stainless steel sculpture "Triple ángulo cilíndrico". 4,00×4,00×2,00m. Torre Picasso. Madrid.

Stainless steel sculpture "Doble prisma vaciado". 3,50×3,50×4,50m. Edificio Puerta de Europa. Madrid.

Stainless steel sculpture. Fundación Antonio Camuñas. Madrid.

Stainless steel and granite sculpture. 3,00×3,00×3,00m. Edificio BBVA. Tres Cantos. Madrid.

Weathering steel sculpture "Doble prisma vaciado". 3,50×3,50×4,50m. Edificio Cajamadrid. Las Rozas. Madrid.

Stainless Steel sculpture "Doble sol contrapuesto". 2,00×2,52×3,58m. Edificio Repsol YPF. Madrid.

Stainless Steel sculpture "Doble sol contrapuesto". 4,00×5,04×7,16m. Centro Tecnológico Repsol YPF. Móstoles. Madrid.

Glass sculpture "Diafragma decafónico de dígitos". 108,00×28,80m. Facade of Instituto Nacional de Estadística building. Madrid.

Stainless Steel sculpture "Primera escultura vacía IV". 0,96×0,96×0,75m. Finca Vallegarcía. Toledo.

Weathering Steel sculpture "Primer helicoide de once prismas cuadrados crecientes 2×1 light". 7,20×15,90×6,00m. Glorieta del ingeniero Angel Pérez Saiz. Cuenca.

www.cruznovillo.com

Index

ISBN 978-0-9935812-3-6

Published by Counter-Print
www.counter-print.co.uk